Benfleet 1933, by H.M. Luyken courtesy of Beecroft Art Gallery, Southend.

SOUTH BENFLEET

A HISTORY

Benfleet on the Thames, c.1900. A drawing by C.W. Wyllie.

SOUTH BENFLEET

A HISTORY

Robert Hallmann

Phillimore

2005

Published by
PHILLIMORE & CO. LTD
Shopwyke Manor Barn, Chichester, West Sussex, England
www.phillimore.co.uk

ISBN 1 86077 359 1

Printed and bound in Great Britain by
CAMBRIDGE PRINTING

Contents

For Minna and Theo

List of Illustrations

Frontispiece: *Benfleet on the Thames*, *c.*1900

Introduction and Acknowledgements

My first acquaintance with South Benfleet was many years ago when I arrived by train to look for a place to settle with a young family. It must have been the salty sea air that day, that hooked me and kept me here as I stepped onto the platform.

An earlier arrival, the Rev. A.C. Holthouse, described his first impression in the parish magazine in 1914 in these terms: 'South Benfleet may not be what is called an ideal village but it is certainly a pretty one. The abundance of beautiful red-tiled houses showing among the green trees, the glimpse of the river ... these are the things which strike one coming here for the first time.'

Benfleet has always had its admirers, from the first Saxon invaders who named it, the Vikings who found it convenient, at least for a while, the rector who left a legacy of music, the saintly vicar who looked after the people in times of illness, to the Nicholsons and their work at the church and Dr Priestley and others who researched its history.

When you look into that history, you meet some fascinating people from the past, for good or bad. When Daniel Defoe made his *Tour through the Eastern Counties of England* early in the 18th century (1722), he related tall tales of marshland farmers who had convinced him that some of them had married 14 and even 15 wives. Not all at once, one presumes. Marsh fever was given as the reason that killed off their spouses.

And I was informed that in the marshes on the other side of the river over against Candy Island there was a farmer who was then living with the five-and-twentieth wife, and that his son, who was but about thirty-five years old, had already had about fourteen.

Defoe mentions Benfleet among a list of places along his journey, running from Fobbing to the Dengie Peninsula.

Was our hoyman James Mathews one of Daniel Defoe's informers? With James's 33 children, the famous writer and traveller was bound to have believed him. Another possible informant comes to mind, the doggerel-writing Revd Dr Francis Clerke, with his sense of humour that placed a stork on a golden background on the gravestone of the said hoyman from Suttons Farm. The dates fit, but the notion will of course have to stay pure, if tantalising, conjecture.

There still remain many questions unanswered. Will it ever be possible to raise some of the old Viking ships from their resting places deep down in the mud of the creek? Did the composer J.C. Mantel ever really live in South Benfleet? In the modern climate of apathy, will St Mary's church survive another 1,100 years?

I should like to thank those lovely people of South Benfleet who shared their stories and their photos during several convivial meetings, when memories flowed like well aged wine ... It's a humbling experience, researching so many lives.

The illustrations in this book are reproduced by kind permission of the following:

Mr and Mrs Amery 33; Derek Barber 7, 24, 26, 40, 49, 59, 60, 67, 68, 71, 75, 76, 77, 79, 80, 89, 93, 96, 103, 110, 111, 112, 123, 125, 131, 147; Jackie Barnes 16, 36, 41, 66, 69, 70, 72, 73, 74, 84, 85, 86, 95, 100, 104, 109, 114, 117, 121, 134, 139, 143, 144, 145, 154, 157; Benfleet Horticultural Society 95; Boyce Hill Golf Club 39, 150; British Library 5, (Music Dept.) 44, 45, 46, 47; Helga Brück 43; Castle Point Borough Council 126, 129, 154, 160; Dean and Chapter of Westminster 13, 14, 17; Jack Dobson 15, 22, 61; Echo Newspapers, 8; Essex County Council Historic Buildings Section 11; Essex County Council Planning Dept. 19; Essex Record Office *frontispiece*, 42, 55, 63, 101, 115, 118, 122, 132, 136, 137; Footsteps 83; Morris Johnson, 78, 120, 149; Margaret Keen 37; John and Paddy Marrison 12, 54, 58, 99, 141; Middleton Press 90; Phillimore 9, 23, 28, 127; Bobby Phillips 58, 65; South Benfleet Primary School 146; Southend Museum 25, 30, 32, 34, 35, 38, 50, 52, 64, 81, 82, 87, 88, 91, 92, 97, 98, 102, 105, 107, 108, 113, 119, 124, 130, 133, 135, 138, 140, 142, 155, 156; Wire Collection, Vestry House Museum, (London Borough of Waltham Forest) 31; V&HV Rolland's Supplement to the Armorial General by J-B Rietstap, Volume II (published by Heraldry Today, Ramsbury, Wiltshire in 1993) 28. Other illustrations are by the author or from the author's own collection.

Sundry map illustrations are by the author, based on maps supplied by Bill Snow of Castle Point Borough Council, especially the Benfleet Tithe Map of 1841. Others are based on ideas by the Benfleet Historical Society and Dr Harold Priestley.

Special thanks are due to Karen Bowman for her diligent research, her reading and image collecting and to Norman Chisman of the Benfleet Historical Society, who read an early version of the manuscript.

Many thanks also to Derek Barber and to Jackie Barnes for their fund of pictures, memorabilia and memories and to all the many people who contributed pictures, maps and memories, including: Mr & Mrs Amery, John and Paddy Marrison and Bobby Phillips, Iris Sugg (née Knightley), Morris and Betty Johnson, Jack Dobson, Pauline Turner and Dudley Hawkins of Benfleet Conservative Club, Margaret Keen, former churchwarden Richard Cerson, Ken and Janet Hegan of Benfleet Camera Club, Frank Tomkins of Benfleet Horticultural Society, Ian Tickell of Boyce Hill Golf & Country Club, Rob Gray of the Benfleet Operatic & Dramatic Society, Joy Turner of Castle Point Borough Council and especially Bill Snow for the loan of maps.

Thanks also to Father Michael Galloway for allowing me access to the vestry in the tower of St Mary's when the collection of past parish magazines was still held there.

Christine Reynolds, Assistant Keeper of the Muniments, Westminster Abbey Muniments Room. Ken Crowe of Southend Museum. Clare Hunt of the Beecroft Art Gallery.

Toby Evans of Southend Central Library. Meriel Kennedy and Jill Henderson of Southend Record Office. The ladies of Essex Record Office. Sally Gale of Essex County Council Historic Buildings Section. [Plan of St Mary's church from the 'Royal Commission on Historical Monuments (England), An Inventory of the Historical Monuments in Essex Volume IV, HM Stationery Office 1923.]

Last, but not least, a big thanks to David Galbraith and Helga Brück, without whom Benfleet's composer J.C. Mantel would have remained in local obscurity.

Note: the author has used original spellings, as appropriate, throughout the book.

I

Out of the Water

The mind struggles when trying to get to grips with the length of time over which the bed of chalk underlying Essex was laid down by the tiny skeletons of sea creatures. This took place when south-east Essex still lay submerged under the ocean and before the tough, impervious London Clay covered it, some fifty million years ago. The clay may be bad news for gardeners, but it is favoured by trees. In places 400 feet thick, it contains fossilised remains of mammals (such as the tapir), turtles and birds, as well as fruits and the seeds of palm trees. Earth movements between ten and thirty million years ago forced these sediments above sea level. Ice sheets never engulfed this area, but streams from the melting ice spread the pebbles and rocks that were ground underneath.

By the end of the last ice age, around 10,000 B.C., most of south Essex was covered by forest. At the tops of the hills we today find leas of lighter soil, sands and gravels laid down as glacial deposits at Thundersley and Hadleigh. Here the soil supported heathland in contrast to the forest all around. The Thames deposits silt as the water slows on its way to the sea and the tides deposit earth as they sweep in, alternately, from the south and north coasts. This silting up with alluvium is responsible for the creation of islands like Wallasea, Foulness, Potton, Rushley, Havengore, New England, Canvey Island – and the Benfleet levels.

In earlier times an area of Benfleet stretching roughly from St Mary's church to Hopes Green and west of Jotmans Farm would have been flooded at high tide and, even at low tide, small boats would have been able to reach as far inland as Hopes Green. Today the primary school marks the site where the stream that flowed down what is now Grove Road entered the creek. A different stream crossed near today's South View Road and there was another just north of the church. Early travellers would have had to avoid lower areas if they wanted to pass between the church and the village while keeping their feet dry. These low marshy levels are thus the reason for Benfleet's main throughfare curving round north and west to Jotmans Lane, where the road continued past St Margaret's church to Pitsea and on. Since the building of the A13 made that route possible, the High Road has veered north at Cemetery Corner, to Tarpots and what is now the London Road. Today the railway line cuts across the levels, but the recreation ground opposite the church still occasionally stands under water. Traces of an earlier sea wall can still be found at the western side of the churchyard.

The creek's constant silting-up explains the claims made for large numbers of ships there in past times, and was eventually responsible for ending Leigh-on-Sea's status as a naval harbour. We must remember that in the Middle Ages ships and barges were still able to reach Hadleigh Castle to the east carrying building stones from Kent. A hundred years earlier the stones for Hadleigh church had arrived in a similar manner. The earlier parts of Benfleet church, too, were built of Kentish ragstone. The

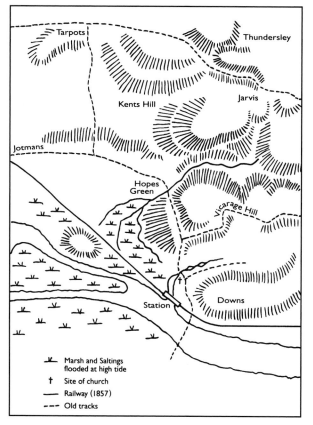

1 *The Creek, marshes and high ground of Benfleet in times past. Tracks and later roads, railway and modern place names are included for guidance. The village formed around the church and Hall Farm was established at the bottom of Vicarage Hill.*

continuous laying down of deposits means that no early human traces can be found unless one digs deep, but on high ground near Badger Hall, off Kiln Road, Mesolithic flints have been found, proof at least of an early human presence.

Celts and Romans

In celtic pre-Roman times, when the Iceni and Trinovantes tribes occupied Norfolk and today's Suffolk respectively, the area roughly north of the Thames was home to the Catuvellauni, and Essex was their eastern extent. In May A.D. 43 the Romans made a second, successful attempt to invade these shores, and the native forces were decisively beaten off between the rivers Medway

and the Thames. The Britons, under Caratacus, son of Cunobelin, retreated across the Thames, pursued by the intruders. It is thought that the crossing point was at nearby Mucking, where at that time it was still possible to cross from sandbank to sandbank at low tide, a useful route for light native forces, but one not necessarily known or possible to the invaders. By the time Emperor Claudius arrived with his elephants, in August or September, the Romans had made a Thames crossing possible at Westminster for his triumphal 'capture' of Colchester. But Benfleet did not remain untouched by Roman influence.

The fabric of Benfleet's old church contains Roman tiles, some in a meaningful cross pattern on one of the buttresses. In the 18th century it was reported that a man 'ditching' a field in the parish of Benfleet found an urn containing 1,500 Roman coins. When a petrol pump was being erected in South Benfleet High Road in 1926, large tiles, which had once been the lining of a Roman well or a spring, were found approximately four to five feet deep. In 1971 Canvey received its second approach road, the A130 from Sadlers Farm roundabout on the outskirts of South Benfleet, which crosses Jotmans Lane and the railway to Waterside Farm roundabout, avoiding human habitations. At the point on the Benfleet side where the road crosses the creek to the island, members of Benfleet Historical Society found fragments of pottery, roof tiles, a bronze pin, bone and unopened shellfish. Finds were identified from the early Iron Age and Roman and Saxon times, and some medieval pottery (shards of jugs and cooking pots) dating as late as the 13th and 14th centuries, was also discovered. In view of the large quantities of coarse pottery it is easy to imagine a settlement near a red hill. According to Warwick Rodwell, who made a study of the finds, fragments of amphorae prove that 'British salt workers were able to consume best Italian wine in the latter part of the Iron Age'. The finds were brought up during the bridge foundation excavations from six to nine feet down, in or

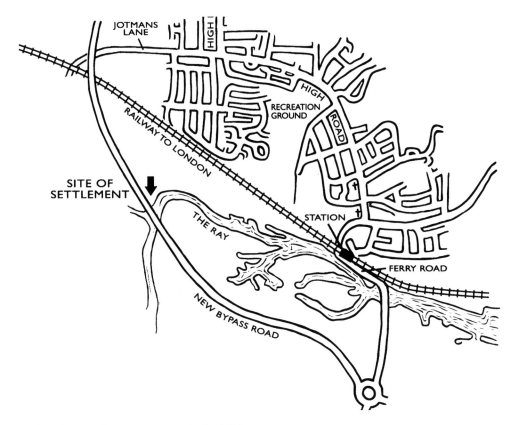

2   *When the new Canvey access road, the A130, was built in 1971, evidence of an earlier occupation was found on the Benfleet side of its route. Archaeology spanned a period of more than a thousand years, from the first to the 14th centuries. The modern planners had followed a similar route to the Romans.*

on blue London clay, and spanned a period of well over a thousand years.

The long-vanished Roman road took a similar route to the new road, running via the heights of North Benfleet, Runwell and Rettendon to the imperial military station at Chelmsford. It is quite probable that what drew the Romans to a creek in South Benfleet was the legions' need for salt, which had been panned along the coast of Essex since Celtic times – as the so-called 'red hills' on Canvey Island bear witness. These raised areas are reminders of this industry, and were formed by the evaporation of salt by fire in large earthenware pans.

The Creekside Village with the Saxon Name

Anglo-Saxons migrated to England about A.D. 500, founding the kingdom of Essex (East Saxa) about A.D. 527. (Aelle and three sons had landed at Selsey in A.D. 477 to found the South Saxon kingdom of Sussex.) By A.D. 630 Benfleet found itself on the edge of the overkingship (*bretwaldaship*) of King Edwin. From A.D. 757–796 it was part of Offa's Kingdom, and from A.D. 802–829 it was part of the overkingship of King Egbert.

The earliest known reference to Benfleet (A.D. 963) is as *Beamfleote* in the Anglo-Saxon Chronicle. Those who first arrived at the place where a stream-fed creek off the river Thames and Hadleigh Ray offered safe anchorage backed by a ring of wooded hills simply named it after what they found – trees and fleet. 'Beam' is still recognisable in its modern German form, *Baum*, and 'fleote' shows evidence of its connection with the word for a flowing stream, *Fluss*.

Later a section of the village expanded inland and became North Benfleet. The two villages have been called Great Benfleet and Little Benfleet and, in Latin, *Benfleet Magna* and *Benfleet Parva*. While South Benfleet has spread inland out of all proportion, however, in North Benfleet time seems to have stood still – it remains an enclave among green fields between the new A130 and Benfleet's New Thundersley to the east, and the ever-approaching Basildon to the west.

There have been many ways of spelling the name of the settlement over the ages. Only with the completion of the London, Tilbury and Southend railway line in 1857 was it finally settled, when the station sign read 'Benfleet'. Hopes Green was *Hope* in *c*.1350 and *Hop(p)eswy(c)k(e)* in 1517, becoming *Hoppes Grene* by 1563. A small landlocked bay that was saltwater at flood tide and freshwater at ebb, it was 'Hoppeswyk' when sheep grazed there, becoming 'Green' when the saltings had been enclosed.

Earlier recorded spellings:

A.D. 963	Beamfleote
1068	Benfleota
1117	Bienflet
1157	Bemflet
1200	Bamflet
1250	Beamfleotam
1272	Boneflet
1291	Bemfeth
1397	Sowthbeniflete
1486	Southbewinflete
1519	Bendflyt
1576	Bemflete
1846	Bemfleet

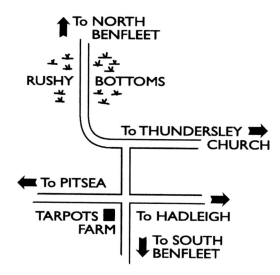

3 *The South and North Benfleet connection.*

II

Vikings and Normans

The Battle of Benfleet

For reasons somewhat different from those of the early Saxon settlers, Vikings established a camp at Benfleet in the ninth century. The creek was ideal for their purpose, providing safe water and dry land just a day's sailing from London with the open sea to the east, and protected by a low island opposite that was regularly flooded and good for little but raising sheep.

The Benfleet camp was shielded by water on three sides. In those days the inlet still reached around what is now the churchyard, crossing what is now the High Road to meet two stream-fed ponds. The rest of the Danish camp, which lay up the slope and south over the brow back down to the Ray, was a safe enclave, well fortified with ditch and rampart; and surmounted by a stockade. It is believed that the rampart followed a line along today's Grosvenor Road on the high ground, crossing

St Mary's Road, before descending to the Ray. A distinct dip in St Mary's Road is thought to mark the line of the earthwork. The Rev. W.E. Heygate reported in 1863 that there was a distinct indentation on the west side of the slope, just behind the present shops opposite the church. This is thought to have marked a special interior fortlet or keep where the leader of the garrison and his bodyguard were housed.

The Danes' veteran leader was the ruthless, if charismatic, Haesten (also recorded as Haestan, Hastein or Hasting). His nicknames, 'Niger', 'the Black', or even 'the African', referred to the fact that around A.D. 860 (as recorded in *Annales bertiniani*) he had left France and with 62 ships had explored as far south and east as the Mediterranean and Morocco. (Some scholars believe they got as far as Alexandria in Egypt.) His journey had started in Scandinavia and he had arrived in France via Ireland. In Steenstrup's

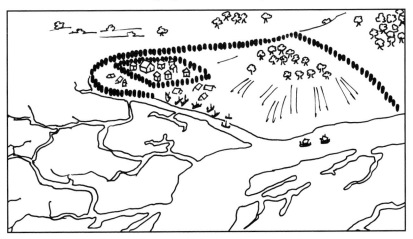

4   *A possible projection of the Viking camp at South Benfleet. Few clues remain today.*

Normannerne (The Normans) Haesten is called 'far-famed' or 'famous'. The Anglo-Saxon Chronicle refers to him as chieftain.

Later, maybe because France had been bled dry or the opposition became too effective, Vikings crossed from Boulogne to Kent in 250 ships, which brought men, women, children, horses and all. They established camps at Appledore in the south and Milton in the north of Kent. But England had a new and effective leader, Alfred of Wessex, who prevented the two camps from joining up. King Alfred was the most effective opponent the Vikings had met anywhere in Europe since the death of Charlemagne in A.D. 810. Essex had been incorporated in the Danelaw in A.D. 878. Place names like Wallasea (the stranger's isle) and Wakering (the land of the Waker or Vikings) attest to the Danish presence. Thundersley is derived from 'Thunar's lea' (the lea or meadow of the God of Thunder).

By A.D. 886 Alfred had recovered London from the Danes. His son Edward was by now proving his kingly qualities and Ethelflaed, the king's eldest daughter, had married Ealdorman Ethelred, king of the Mercians, Alfred's staunchest and most reliable ally, who was in charge of London. In 892 Haesten came to Benfleet with 80 ships by which time the Benfleet camp had been established. Another Viking army sailed down from Northumbria into the Straits of Dover in A.D. 893 and turned west towards Devon and Cornwall. Alfred left Kent to confront them. The eastern Danes reassembled at Benfleet, and Ethelred and his Londoners now joined Edward and headed east to face the Benfleet army.

> The fortress at Beamfleote had ere this been constructed by Haesten and he was at the same time gone out to plunder and the Great Army was therein. Then they (the English) came thereto and put the Army to flight and stormed the fortress and took all that was within it, as well as women and children also, and brought the whole to London and all the ships they either broke

5 *Benfleet's mention in the Anglo-Saxon Chronicle.*

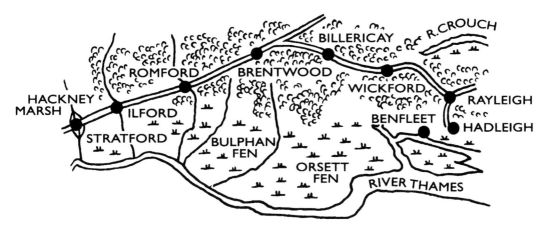

6 *The likely route followed by King Alfred's men, using the cover of wooded high ground as they approached the Viking settlement.*

in pieces or burned or brought to London and Rochester, and they brought the wife of Haesten and his two sons to the King ...

Those are the words of the Anglo-Saxon Chronicle, recorded some seventy years after the battle by Ethelweard, King Alfred's elder brother Ethelred's great-grandson. The surprise must have been total and the result was a complete rout. Haesten, the great survivor, who was by then in his early seventies, was conveniently absent at the time.

Alfred demonstrated his kingship by showing mercy towards Haesten's family, whom he apparently returned to the raider. What survivors there were regrouped at Shoeburyness to the east, but many dragonships and seafarers must still be buried deep in Benfleet mud. (Long has there been a legend on Canvey and thereabouts of the headless ghost of a Viking in search of his lost ship.) In 1885 a Mr Spurrell noted: 'sunken ships remain in the fleet close to the camp to this day, for during the construction of the Railway Bridge there some 30 years ago, the navvies came across ships, many of which were charred, and in and about them lay great quantities of human skeletons.' Alas, none of these finds survived.

On the specially secured inner walled area of the Danish camp it is thought that an earlier version of the present church was built, as was often the case when a grateful population thanked God for their deliverance.

It is likely that this early church would have resembled St Peter *ad murum* at Bradwell. There are remains of older foundations to the south-east of the present chancel, as recorded by Sir Charles Nicholson in the 1920s. The National Monuments Record database mentions the finding of a 10th-century coin from Kashmir, which may be evidence of later Viking activity in the area. In 1996 a bronze coin, which has been dated to the Byzantine Empire between A.D. 850 and 950, was found during house extensions in Hall Farm Road, Benfleet, just north of the former Viking enclosure – and on the route the victors would have followed after the Battle of Benfleet on their return west to London.

As for Haesten, he seems to have returned to France. Dudo reports that he made peace with the King of France and took up living quarters there. When a new fleet of Danes gathered at Choisy, Haesten, 'the origin of all evil', joined the King's ambassadors in asking the newcomers' intentions, after which they were curtly rebuffed. The old rake then asked them: 'Did you ever learn about a certain Haesten who was your countryman and went over here with many warriors?'

7   *More than a thousand years ago the ray would have been wider and deeper and the ships would have been Viking longboats.*

The answer was: 'Yes, he started well but his end was no good'.

Benfleet in Domesday Book

In late Saxon and Norman times the unit of local administration was called a Hundred (a division of shires), the origins of which are somewhat obscure. It may have been based on an area occupied by a hundred family groups, or one containing a hundred hides (units of cultivated land of roughly 120 acres). Disputes were settled and offenders judged at the court of 'Hundred Moot'.

Benfleet was part of Barstable Hundred, one of five such districts along Thames-side Essex, together with the hundreds of Rochford, Chafford, Havering Liberty and Becontree. Barstable Hundred encompassed Shenfield and Doddinghurst to the north-west, Chadwell and Tilbury in the south and South Benfleet and Thundersley to the east. Today Barstable is part of Basildon, yet it was there that men from South Benfleet joined others from all around the Hundred in their Court to give evidence together with their priests to the investigators

and clerks who had been charged by William the Conqueror to record what land each man held, how it was stocked and what it was worth, including its worth during King Edward the Confessor's reign.

At least part of the parish of Benfleet belonged to the nuns of St Mary at Barking in the reign of Edward the Confessor. Following the murder of the nuns and the abbey's

8   *Coin found in Hall Farm Road, South Benfleet, in 2004. It has been identified as Byzantine Empire A.D. 850-950. (enlarged)*

destruction by Vikings, it was rebuilt in A.D. 930, and both Benfleet's church and manor were granted to the Abbey of St Mary. After 1066 William the Conqueror gave Benfleet to the Abbey of Westminster instead. 'Hundred of Barstable. In [South] Benfleet, St Peter's has 7 hides and 30 acres, which lay in [the lands of] St Mary's Church before 1066; but King William gave the church with the land to St Peter's, Westminster…' records Domesday Book in 1086. An eighth hide had been handed to St Martin's le Grand in London by one Engelric, apparently without the King's knowledge, so it would probably have been handed back to St Peter's.

Lord of that manor was the Abbot of Westminster. The survey also tells us there were 15 villagers (villeins) and the number of smallholders (bordars) had risen from seven before the Conquest to twelve. There was pasture for 200 sheep (part of this manor lay in Canvey), though there were actually only 50, and only three pigs, which would indicate a lack of woodland. The woodland lay on higher ground and would become part of the Royal Forest. Some ninety years later, in 1157, the grant was confirmed by the only English Pope, Adrian IV (1154-9). There were no freemen and no serfs, but other men held farms of the abbey. The survey informs us that there were two ploughs, with a further five belonging to the men. Eight oxen were reckoned to a plough, so the Abbot of Westminster had 16 oxen and the villagers had 40 between them. They would have about 30 acres each, but, as bondsmen, they owed three days' work a week to the bailiff of the manor and they had to plough half the lord's land first (half lay fallow each year) before they could start on their own. They were, however, entitled to pass on their holdings to their heirs. Bordars had small plots of four to eight acres and their services to the manor were more diverse and plentiful. The Domesday survey did not concern itself with personal servants, clerks, women or children. Also lodged in St Peter's, Westminster, were 50 acres at Bowers Gifford, 'which one Englishman holds'. While the Benfleet estate was valued at £6, the one at Bowers was listed as being worth 20 shillings.

Swein (Sweyne), a relative of King William I, held two manors in the present Castle Point district. The land 'which Alwin, a free man, held before 1066', of two hides (240 acres), was worked by five smallholders and two serfs, and there were 250 sheep in pasture. This may be the land which later became the Jarvis estate. The pasture probably lay in Canvey, where many parishes in the area sent their sheep for the summer. Of Alwin's three ploughs only one was left by 1086, but, Domesday Book notes, 'One plough can be restored'. Swein's other estate was Thundersley, a manor of five hides and 15 acres, which had been owned by a Saxon called Godric, a King's thane, before Swein grabbed it, as he did Rayleigh, Hockley, Eastwood, Prittlewell and others. Thundersley (*Thunresleam*) was recorded as holding pasture with 200 sheep and woodland for 50 swine. The manor and the villagers held two ploughs each. The manor of Thundersley came into the possession of Edward II in 1313.

The land Harold held before 1066, of eight hides (960 acres), with 21 villagers and six

---

/ TERRA sci petri de Weftmonafterio .   Hund de bdeftapla .
In Benflet ħt Sc̄s Petrus. VII . hid . 7 . XXX . ac . que jacebant in eccła sc̄æ
mariæ t . r . e . f; rex . W . dedit ecclam cū tr̄a sc̄o petro . de Weftmonafterio
jn q̄ tr̄a ſt . II . car . iŋ dn̄io . 7 . v . car hom̄ ; sep̄ . xv . uilt . Tc̄ . VII . bor . m̄
XII . Paftur . cc . ou . m̄ . dim̄ . moł . Tc̄ uał . IIII . lib . m̄ . vI . Octauā hid de
ead eccła sc̄æ mariæ . dedit Ingelric sc̄o martino . 7 adhuc ibi ē ut confu
lat teftat fine juffu regis .

9 *Benfleet in Domesday Book.*

smallholders, 30 acres of woodland and pasture for 130 sheep, is thought to be North Benfleet. 'Now Ranulf brother of Ilger has charge of this manor in the King's hand,' it says, showing that it had changed hands from King Harold to William I. While South Benfleet was held of Westminster Abbey, North Benfleet was held of the King. The two manors shared one mill between them, which was probably tidal and lay in Benfleet Creek.

Confusingly, a fourth Benfleet estate of one hide (120 acres) is mentioned as lying in the hundred of Wibertsherne (Dengie peninsula), which a Saxon freeman called Leofhard lost to Theodoric Pointel. By 1086 there was just one smallholder and pasture for 40 sheep, but under Leofhard there had also been one plough and a fishery.

The marshes of Canvey, opposite *Benfleet Magna*, were shared by several owners and parishes. Long before the island was secured by the Dutch, the area had to be protected and there is proof that embanking was already taking place. In 1376 the Abbess of Barking paid for the repair of breaches in the sea wall and in 1437 the Abbey of Christchurch, Canterbury, made good 154 perches (*c*. 800 yards) around its land on Canvey. After 1066 Westminster Abbey would similarly have protected its Benfleet manor.

The Church and the Abbey Manor

The original small church, which very probably rose in the aftermath of the Battle of Benfleet of A.D. 893, as Sir Charles Nicholson suggested, would have been led by a priest sent by the nuns of St Mary's, Barking Abbey. This may be the origin of the local tradition that there once was a monks' cell here. The beginnings of the present church date from soon after the Norman Conquest, in a much reduced version of today's building. The parish magazine of February 1928 carried a likely description of that early church of about A.D. 1200. Imagine a wide nave without pillars, but probably a small semi-circular apse with a narrow arch between nave and chancel,

'two narrow windows with horn rather than expensive glass', a bell turret instead of a tower, with a thatched roof. As in other old churches, the plastered walls would have been covered with instructive paintings of biblical scenes and saints. The rough floor would not have wooden seats but rush matting or straw. Today's church grew from those beginnings. Over the centuries it was heightened and enlarged with north and south aisles, tower and chancel.

More land in South Benfleet was granted to Westminster Abbey, particularly in Norman days. Peter de Fantone made a grant in 1250, and John Pecche and John Thurston in 1354. Thomas Ashe and Simon Barton gave 142 acres. The manor and the farms leased out by the Abbey of Westminster provided extra food and beer for the monks. Sometime before 1214, when the new Abbot Ralph de Rundle took charge, control of the manor was handed down to the prior and the monks. They took turns to go in procession on the feast days of St Laurence, St Vincent, St Nicholas and St Benedict. On those days wine instead of beer was provided in the abbey refectory; the custom arose that 'whenever a little extra was provided' for the monks on feast days by way of victuals, it was 'the revenues from the marshes belonging to the South Benfleet manor' that paid for it.

Many documents concerning the everyday working of the estate are to be found in the Muniments Room of Westminster Abbey. They name people to whom lands were conveyed and others who made gifts to the Abbey. Many of them carried the surname 'de Benfleet'. Among them are Algar (1210), Bartholomew (1219) and his sons Salomon (1250) and William, Alexander (1263), Stephen (1280) and Osward (1300). A John de Benfleet, described as a chaplain, held a marsh called Sandflete of '100 acres of arable land and adjacent pasture' in 1290, which he let out to Gilbert Coleman for eight cheeses ... and 'the fishing in the Flete'. Before his death in May 1298 he had lost his lands to the king. Benfleet people seem to have occupied themselves with tilling the land, shepherding

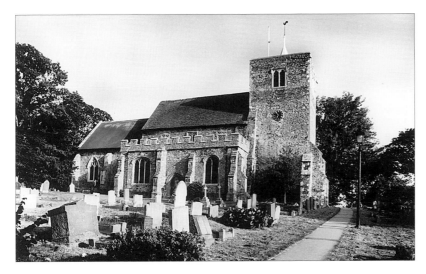

10 *St Mary's church.*

sheep on the marshes – including Canvey Island – and making cheeses from sheep's milk for export to London, as well as fishing, gathering rushes and felling trees.

Land transfer, through sale or inheritance, was handled by the manor court. In earlier days the symbol of ownership, the rod in the form of an actual piece of turf from the land, was handed first to the lord, then by him to the buyer. John Attwood senior came to the court in 1415, 'who holds from the lord by court roll a messuage [dwelling, yard etc.] and 30 acres of land with appurtenances called Tarpodys … The lord grants it to him by manor roll and to his heirs and assigns by the rod, in perpetuity.' The 'Fine' or transfer fee was 8d. One of Attwood's neighbours was admitted as a tenant in 1424: 'At this court was granted by the lord's hand one parcel of land to Henry Baker commonly called the Hyde containing by estimation, hedged and ditched 30 acres and lying below the land of William Garland and John Attwood called Tarpottys which is one foot from the King's highway leading to South Benfleet from Bowers and abutting on Tarpots Lane …'

On 20 March 1360 a document from 'the Abbot and Convent of Westminster' stated that they would celebrate the anniversary of Nicholas Lytlyngton the prior from the profits of the manor of Hyde, lands in Knightsbridge and marshlands in South Benfleet. 'There shall be distributed on that day to the poor the sum of half a mark [6s. 8d.] and also three shillings and four pence for the recreation of the Boy Bishop and his companions.' This curious report refers to the custom of selecting boy bishops to reign from St Nicholas' day (6 December) to Holy Innocents' day (28 December) and suggests that Hyde Park, Knightsbridge and South Benfleet paid for the celebration.

Tithes and the Land

Benfleet's vicar was and is appointed by Westminster Abbey. The earliest known was John de Cornubiensis (1189-98). The priest collected the tithes annually, 'the great tithes – those on corn, hay and wool going to the Abbey, and the small tithes on everything else, being granted to the Vicar who also had a small holding of his own called the Glebe.' (School Lane used to be called Glebe Lane and a tithe barn survived into the last century.) The South Benfleet manor rolls in 1424 mention the return of the vicar's lands to the abbey on his death: 'And since John Fyllo, Vicar of the Church in Benfleet (1390-1424) is dead since the last court, according to the custom of the manor, the land held is returned to the hands of the lord.'

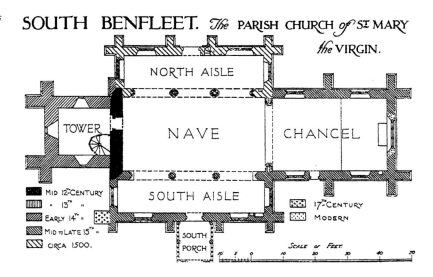

11 *Plan of St Mary's church fabric and expansion since the 12th century.*

Suttons or South Downs

One of the most important gifts to the Abbey had been that of Suttons Farm. The De Heveningham family of Eastwood owned it in 1300. Eventually they sold it to Roger Bassett, who, in 1392, gave it to the Abbey. Early in the 15th century Suttons was held by Thomas Blosme and was called Southdowne. The farm occupied both sides of the Downs and was one of the most important in the parish. The large burial slab of Thomas Blosme (+1440) and his wife Olive lies beneath the chancel floor of St Mary's church. In his last will, written in Latin in the time of Henry VI – the will was read on 24 March 1440 – he left another wife, Margery, and a son, William, who was still under age.

A daughter Christina had passed away already. One of the witnesses to the will was Lawrence Richards, vicar of Benfleet (*southbemflete*). The largesse handed out to his 'feoffees' and others points to a man of some considerable substance. His manservant received a pension: 'John Gynes my servant, 1p. per day paid annually, for life.' He also made provision for 'tithes formerly forgotten, 50s.' Among the retinue of 39 lances and 119 archers of Sir William Bourchier at the battle of Agincourt on 25 October 1415 was a likely relative, one Robert Blosme, according to the Battle Roll.

Brass-rubbing enthusiast Jack Dobson, a member of the Monumental Brass Society, removed enough of the floor of the chancel in

12 *Hall Farm on the High Road (Old London Road) with Bridge Houses and church, early in the 20th century.*

13 *Receipt from the Abbot of Colchester for moneys paid by Benfleet via the Abbot of Westminster. 'Acquittance from Frater Gilbert de Polstede, Monk, in the name of (Robert de Grinstead) Abbat of Colec. (Colchester, Co. Essex) (Collector of the tenth imposed for 3 years by Pope Boniface VIII towards the relief of the Roman (Church)) to (Walter de Wenlock) abbat of Westminster for 13s. 4d. from Great Bemflet Church and for 16d. from a pension in Southbemf. for both terms of the 3rd year. Dat. at Colec. XI. Kal. Jun. (22 May) A.D. 1304.'*

14 *'Grant from Simon (Langham) Abbat and the Convent of Westminster to Frater Nicholas de Lytlyngton, Prior of Westminster, that on his decease they will celebrate his anniversary on St Nicholas' day (6 Dec.) each year, also that from the outgoings of La Hyde Manor (Co. Middl.) and of lands and rents formerly belonging to John Conuers in Knyghtebrugge (Knightsbridge, Co. Middl.) and of marshland in Southbemflet (South Benfleet, Co. Essex) (all which Abbey) be distributed to the poor 6s. 8d. and 3s. 4d. for the recreation of the Boy Bishop and his companions. Also ... Dat. in Westminster Chapter House, 20 March, A.D. 1360.' (Abbot's seal on left, the larger Abbey seal on right.)*

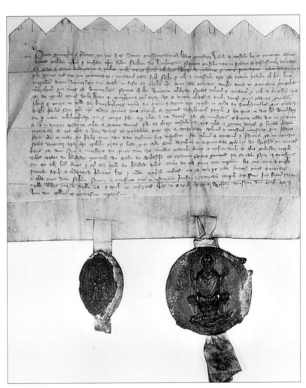

May 1978 (with permission from the Rev. A. Banks), to uncover what must be the largest slab of a bracket brass in Essex. It is nine feet long and four feet wide. The Blosme slab had been described in 1727, before the chancel was laid out in marble at the behest of the Rev. Francis Clerke, but even then the lower descriptive brass panel was missing. The slab was located with the help of Jackie Barnes and her metal detector. The main indents are of a civilian and his wife, though not much of the brass and the rivets has survived. Some fragments were traced to the

Colchester Castle Museum and have since been replaced in situ, together with others found in various places.

In 1654 the manor court was conducted by the steward on behalf of the lords of the manor, the Dean and Chapter of Westminster Abbey. The document mentions land transfers and the allotment of various parcels of land: '...To John Cox of London, Suttons Farm, formerly held by Francis Scott of Fobbing and his wife Elizabeth.' Poynetts, on the Downs east of Suttons, extended into Hadleigh parish. It traces

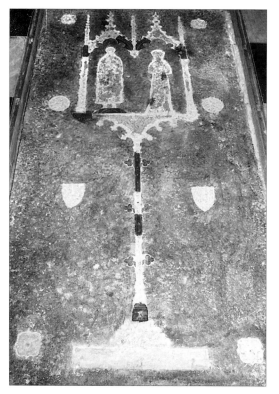

15   *The defaced funeral slab of Thomas Blosme and his wife under the chancel floor of St Mary's church, c.1440.*

its name to John Poynaunt from about 1308. Later it became an endowment for the benefit of the Free Grammar School in Enfield. In 1621 'an estate in the parishes of South Benfleet, Hadley and Thundersley was acquired by Enfield Parish and by a deed of 1621 a trust was set up to administer the rents for the maintenance of a newly built Free Grammar School for the children of inhabitants of the parish and to pay an annual salary of £20 to the schoolmaster...' Equally, Little Tarpots land was a charity in aid of East Hanningfield church. Kents Hill Farm and Sweet Briars were possessions of the Dean and Chapter. Sweet Briars is today a site next to the police station.

Land Ownership

Over the years the old Norman feudal system slackened. By 1650, instead of working on the lord's land a number of days a week, feudal tenants paid a quitrent (a rent paid to be quit or free of personal service). Manorial tenants by then could sell their land, but the quitrent transferred to the new owner. In addition a fine (transfer fee) was paid to the lord at every transfer through death or any other cause.

16   *Sweet Briar farmhouse, now the site of maisonettes next to the Police Station in the High Road.*

III

Medieval and Tudor Benfleet

Following the dissolution of the monasteries Henry VIII handed the lands of St Peter's Abbey to the Dean and Chapter of Westminster, making 'the manors of Bonvyles and Benflete, alias South Beymflete' part of their endowment. (Bonvilles later features in the will of Francis Clerke.) 'Queen Elizabeth confirmed to them [Westminster], 21 May 1560, the Maners of Benflete, alias South Benflete, Monkeflete, Shereswicke, Hoppeswicke, and Sanderswicke.' (Wicks were pasture with milking sheds.) At the same time the Queen added the rectory and advowson of the vicarage, which they still hold today. Under the ownership of Westminster, that combination of accessible safe waterside, freshwater streams, fertile if heavy soil, and the forestry resources of the wooded valleys to the north and east, meant that by the 16th and 17th centuries Benfleet had become one of the busiest ports in Essex. Timber from Shipwrights Wood, Jarvis Wood, West Wood, for example, was shipped to other shipbuilding yards along the coast, as well as to Westminster.

In 1621 Sir Henry Appleton of Jarvis Hall and seven other landowners sought out Dutch merchant Joas Kroppenburg (Croppenbergh, citizen and haberdasher) of London to drain the Canvey marshes and construct the great embankment ('… to gain and recover from the inundacion & overflowing of the River of Thames all the ground & soyle scituate lying & beinge in the Island… it should be lawfull to & for the said Joas Croppenbergh & co, to have free liberty of ingresse & to digg turfe earth gravell

17 *The Westminster Abbey arms since 1560. In 1222 the Abbey had been decreed directly subject to the Pope; in 1534 Henry VIII transferred jurisdiction from the Pope to the Crown. He dissolved the Benedictine Abbey in 1540 and designated it as a cathedral. Queen Mary brought back the monks for three years up to 1559. Elizabeth I constituted the present Collegiate Church under royal authority on 21 May 1560. (Coat of Arms: A gold cross on a blue background with five martlets – birds that never land – the Arms of Edward the Confessor.)*

15

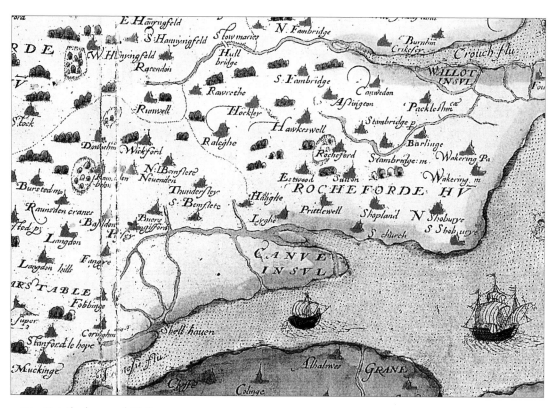

18   *Detail of map of 1576.*

& stones.'). Croppenbergh employed a family relation, the engineer Cornelius Vermuyden, whose work was so outstanding that in 1628 he was knighted by Charles I and became Sir Cornelius Vermuyden. The island had largely been reclaimed by 1623 and the Dutch engineers received a third of the land in payment – 491 acres, 120 rods. The Dutch immigrant workers, in turn, received a part of their pay in land. By 1628 the Dutch population of Canvey numbered some 200 workers, enough to appeal to the King to be allowed their own church in which to worship in Dutch. Permission was granted. Curiously, this eventually led to fisticuffs when the indigenous English population demanded the right to be allowed to worship there also.

Not all obligations were on the Benfleet side. The Session Rolls for Epiphany 1651 state the case of Peter Prim and Anthony Richards of 'Candy Island'. They were taken before the

Grand Jury for 'not repairing the horse dam in the parish of South Benfleet leading into Candy Island, containing about 40 perches'.

In 1712 Bishop Compton came from London at the behest of the Rev. Edward Roberts to consecrate a new English St Katherine's chapel which had been built on the island. This itself was replaced, in 1745, by one dedicated to St Peter.

In time the Dutch intermarried and there are Dutch names among Benfleet's congregation and churchwardens over the next generations. The Vandevords were buried in Benfleet's churchyard 1724–37. John Vandevord was a stalwart member of the South Benfleet Vestry from at least 1708 until 1737, much of the latter years as churchwarden. He may have shared that office with a son, as in 1733 he was referred to as 'senior'. There are several occurrences where the mark of someone with that name appears. This particular John Vandevord's name also alternates with a Thomas Vandeford;

once they even served together. The variety of spellings of this family's name are noteworthy – Vanderwood, Vandiford, Vandevoord and Vandevorde. In the 19th century the Vandervords, then of Southend, owned and sailed some 33 Thames sailing barges.

Peasants and Pilgrims

Benfleet was just a cluster of buildings huddled about the church and along East Street, with a 'common' opposite the *Blue Anchor*, the narrow lane and some isolated cottages. From the church northwards, following Church Street – now the High Road – across a bridge, the road passed the Vicarage and Hall Farm and thence to Hopes Green, Jotmans Lane and eventually to London via Pitsea. Behind Hall Farm lay the Green, where a toy fair was held on 24 August every year. Opposite the Hall a very steep and narrow cutting – formerly Parson's Hill, now Vicarage Hill – climbed east and on to the high ground to Hadleigh and Prittlewell.

The village was a cul-de-sac, culminating in the quay, a beach-like area called 'the Hard', where boats were laid up, similar to many quiet East Anglian corners even today – picturesque, but businesslike, where over many generations locals had spread cartloads of gravel as a base for their boats. This is difficult to imagine today since the road and railway and, more recently, the underpass to Canvey Island have cut off Church Creek from the tide. Now the creek is little more than the grassy bank of a brook. In 1559, however, wharfage was charged at the then quite considerable sum of £20 p.a. (See Maritime Benfleet page 23)

The *Anchor Inn* is shown in the 1770 Register of Ale-houses as the *Blue Anchor*. It was and is a very handsome building of fine timber, originally erected by Westminster craftsmen in about 1380. It is thought to have been a stopover for pilgrims departing for Kent and Canterbury on their way to the shrine of the Blessed Saint Thomas. Perhaps surprisingly, the *Blue Anchor* building originally faced north towards the Hall. Ornate medieval windows found during renovations in 1989 were facing the stables across a yard, which means that today's

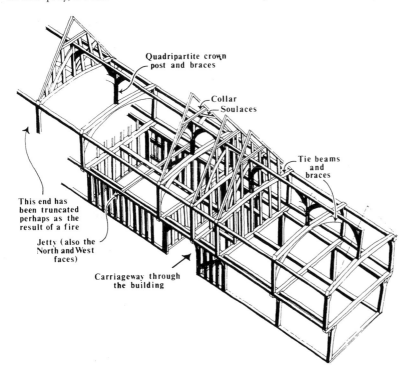

Quadripartite crown post and braces

Collar
Soulaces

Tie beams and braces

This end has been truncated perhaps as the result of a fire

Jetty (also the North and West faces)

Carriageway through the building

19 Anchor *timber frame of c.1381. Sketch by the Essex County Council Planning Department.*

20   *The* Anchor *was white-washed again during the renovations of 1989, as it would have been originally.*

simple frontage used to be the back of the building. At one time a passage led through the main building in the manner of coaching inns. A beautiful 14th-century crownpost roof of four major and two secondary bays in substantial oak timber was found when workmen broke through the second-floor ceiling. Seventeenth-century painting was discovered on the underside of the tie beams. Exposed first-floor joists can now be seen from the bar. The Essex County Council historic buildings section dated the building by its jointing to about 1380. A child's fingerprints, possibly 600 years old, were found when original plaster was removed from internal walls. Given the timescale, erecting the *Anchor* coincided with the Peasants' Revolt of 1381, probably as a courthouse or manor court to replace the manor hall, which is thought to have been destroyed at that time. A skeleton minus hands and feet, most likely of a convicted criminal who could not be interred in sacred ground, was found in 1973 when a service trench was excavated at what was once the rear of the building between the *Anchor* and the War Memorial.

From the *Anchor* the road turned west to the 'Hard', and south-east for the journey on to Canvey (also Candy) Island, a route which rose over the Downs (today's School Lane), then descended steeply down to the causeway. Houses stood on either side of the church gate on the churchyard side. If we reckon that would not leave much space for travellers in the High Road, the renovations at the *Anchor* also sprang another surprise. It was found that, for some reason quite likely connected to the problems of road traffic, a western section of the building has at some time been truncated.

Benfleet's manor hall stood near today's Methodist Church to the south of the High Road, opposite the bottom of Vicarage Hill. The earliest surviving manor rolls date from 1407. The manor hall's replacement would again have been occupied by the bailiff.

The Poll Tax revolt started in Fobbing and eventually spread to London where the Chancellor of the Exchequer was among those who lost their lives. Many manor halls were burnt to destroy the manor rolls which were deemed to be evidence of servitude. Among other repercussions in South Benfleet was the case of Thomas Spragge of South Benfleet 'and others of the same place', who were tried in Chelmsford before Judge Tresilian.

St Mary's Church

St Mary the Virgin church has been developed and added to over the years. Much of the fabric dates from *c*.1400-1500 and comprises flints from the fields, grey Kentish ragstone, white chalky clunch and assorted bricks of various ages. Even Roman bricks and tiles were re-used, indicating at least a former Roman presence in the neighbourhood.

The strong, stocky tower from the 1300s with angle buttresses at the foot and topped by a party-hat spire from the 1700s, holds six bells. The largest, of 1636, is also the oldest. Others date from 1664, 1676 and 1790. The latest, the treble, was added in 1949 to commemorate Peace after the Second World War.

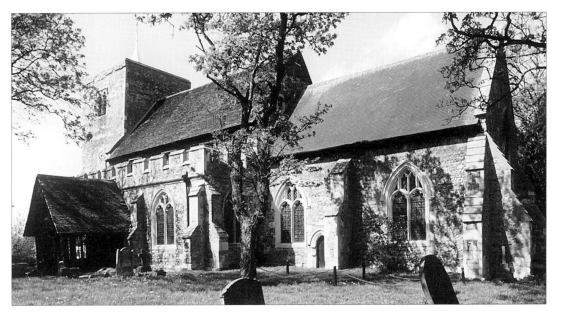

21 *St Mary the Virgin church.*

22 *The six bells of St Mary's, here in the up position, ready to be rung. The largest and oldest of 1636 is the tenor, 3½ ft. in diameter and weighing 11¾ cwt (bottom right). The newest is the treble (second from left, bottom row), added in 1949 to commemorate the Peace.*

Dating from late in the 15th century, the south porch has been called the glory of St Mary's, a beautiful specimen of carved oak and an architectural tour-de-force. The single hammerbeam roof, blind tracery of the front-gable panelling and the deep and finely cut traceries of the eight lights on each side are considered especially successful.

Benfleet and the Law

The system of local government after William the Conqueror, the manor court, would have been held in Benfleet at Hall Farm under the bailiff, outside if weather permitted, or otherwise in the lord's barn, where the officials, the clerk and 12 'jurors' faced the villagers. In 1412 the 12 just villagers serving as jurors were Robert Miller, John Sawold, John Brown, Thomas Rede, John

Hubard, Adam Nash, John Shalmond, Thomas Odam, John Gerveys, John Geffrey, Thomas Botyll and Thomas Boys. (Allowing for spelling discrepancies, one might recognise local names such as Reed, Jarvis and Boyce … .) Fines for such misdemeanour as neglecting tenements, not scouring roadside ditches, or assaulting the constable could amount to 1d. or 2d., the assault on a manor official rating at 8d.

In 1439 Benfleet was reported as having 50 men capable of bearing arms, so it is quite endearing to think of this quiet if busy medieval backwater facing problems far removed from the world stage. In 1415, the year of the battle of Agincourt, here in Benfleet Thomas Hey was

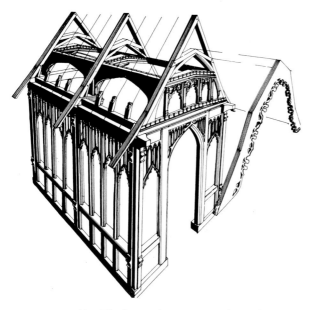

23   *The late 15th-century south porch.*

24   *The south porch in 1912-14.*

taken to task for not cleaning his section of a ditch that ran to both sides of the roads: 'The jury present that Thomas Hey has a certain ditch on Church Street which has not been cleaned out.' The manor rolls record that he was fined two pence. It was the task of the surveyor of highways to bring villagers to book when they did not carry out their civic duty and clean out their section of the draining ditches. The Highway Act of 1555 demanded that the Vestry of every parish had to choose two surveyors of the highways from lists submitted to the justices every year.

Owners occasionally had to be reminded of their obligations: Session Rolls of Epiphany 1603 carry the following item: '…We present the landholders of South Benfleet Hall for not laying a bridge in the salt marsh in the common footpath leading from south Benfleet to Pitsea, Bowers [Gifford] and Vange, very noisome to the Queen's liege people that go that way.' The people holding land from the Abbey were dilatory, it seems. In return, Westminster honoured its obligations: £20 for 'bricks and tiles made in Benfleet' for church repairs were paid by a Westminster Abbey official to Roger Appleton of Jarvis Hall in 1607, according to the manor rolls.

If all else failed, the surveyors themselves might have to be taken to court, as the 1706 Quarter Sessions lists of defaulters demonstrate: 'James Snesher, Yeoman and … Ballard of South Benfleet before and since 17th August were Surveyors of the Highways there and neglecting the Execution of their Office allowed the Highway leading from 'Downes' in South Benfleet to Canvey Island to remain in Decay through want of Repair. Witness Henry Appleton.' (36 years later, on 14 May 1742, Canvey, 'a day's work for a cart, three horses and two men cost 6s. 6d.'. On 5 July the same year, '2 days' work to heighten causeway road from Benfleet, 2 carts, 4 horses, 3 men at £1'. Drink was paid to the value of one shilling. 'For a new footbridge over the creek into the island £14. 13s. 8d.')

25   *Hall barn and farm, on the left of picture from the creek, c.1923. The old house between the churchyard and the creek has also long gone.*

26   *Hay from Canvey Island would be transferred onto barges (hoys), destined for London's horses, c.1910.*

An Act of Parliament stipulated in 1572 that every parish must have two overseers of the poor. As the surveyors were empowered to levy highway rates, so the overseers could levy poor rates. This could be for housing, clothing, food, heating in winter, for example. In the era before the National Health Service it was the village's responsibility to look after those who could not afford their own medicine, doctor or hospital. A receipt of 1684 states that Marinius Reinolds, overseer of the poor of South Benfleet, paid the sum of two shillings and ten pence to Peter English for 'a Cure done upon William Marsh a poore Man'. The parish dealt with the problem of illness by engaging a doctor on an annual basis. Dr Seacole of Prittlewell was the first to be so engaged, in 1796 for a fee of ten guineas a year. A memo of Easter 1800 explains: 'Mr Dobson agrees to attend the Poor of this Parish as Surgeon and Midwife at the Sum of £12 per annum including Accidents of every Kind and Denomination whatever.'

More serious misdemeanours were dealt with at Sessions Courts held in Chelmsford. Session Rolls of Midsummer 1565 recorded the indictment of Thomas Draper of South Benfleet, 'for breaking into the close of John Dagnett at South Benfleet, with dogs and nets, and hunting and taking the rabbits belonging to John Stephen, and also assaulting the same John Dagnett'.

In 1576 South Benfleet received a legacy of £6 13s. 4d. (10 marks) under the will of John Letton, a yeoman parishioner. This substantial sum was handed over with the judge's instruction that 'they shall have a bible of the largest volume, a communion cup and all the other necessary books, and to repair the churchyard'.

Some incidents might have more permanent consequences as when a South Benfleet 'labourer there committed fornication with Mary Todma spinster. Witnesses: Thomas Hatch. Ezra Hatch'.

The manor farm's barn was the setting for a birth one winter's night at the end of the 16th century. Benfleet's historian Dr Harold Priestley illuminated the barn's history with the poignant story of 'Edward Prentis, a herdsman employed by Henry Appleton', who entered the barn of the Manor Hall to find 'a woman lying on a heap of straw, a newly-born babe in her arms'. The herdsman's wife in a nearby cottage with her own 13-month-old baby Gabriel took in and looked after the child. The parish register noted: 'ffebruary 12. 1593 was baptised Sara, daughter of Margaret, a Vagrant Person that was brought to Bed in the Hall Barn whose husband she said was buried in Colchester…'

In 1696 the inhabitants of South Benfleet were indicted because from 16 June to 14 July they had 'not repaired a common footpath there leading from Bowers Gifford to South Benfleet church'.

Local Administration

In Benfleet we have seen the Manorial Hall destroyed and the *Anchor* building erected as a focal point of the legal system following the Peasants' Revolt, under a representative of the lords of the manor – though some decisions were taken by the lords of the Jarvis estate.

In the 16th century power began to shift from the manor court to the church and to elected local representatives headed by the churchwardens. In 1654 in South Benfleet, though, the lords of the manor were still the Dean and Chapter of Westminster Abbey. The Manor Court was conducted by the steward on their behalf. It is the last occasion we know of when the steward made local legal decisions.

The South Benfleet Vestry Minutes Book starts at Easter 1679 and offers an interesting insight into the way such self-government worked. Village elders – and later sometimes women – were elected yearly at Vestry meetings, taking on the posts of 'Overseer of the Poor', 'Surveyor of Highways' and 'Constables' under the leadership of the 'Churchwarden'. This system had its imperfections, but it reflects continuity through the generations. It operated in a time of stability, as is evident from the many names in that Vestry Book which can still be found on gravestones and family tombs in the churchyard.

Maritime Benfleet

A sawyer's pit of several feet of sawdust was found opposite the *Anchor* public house and the War Memorial during building excavations for an extension to the Off Licence premises. Logs would have been cut into planks and beams here by two men, one of whom stood in the pit underneath the timber. Finds included broken clay pipes and lots of oystershells, the poor man's fish and chips. Together with the sawmill beside the creek they are testimony to past industry in that area.

The broad, flat-bottomed 'hoy' was the favourite carrier and, together with 'helmet', meaning quay, it gives its name to one of South Benfleet's three ancient public houses, the 15th-century *Hoy* (it became the *Hoy and Helmet* in the 20th century). More convenient than the *Blue Anchor* and the *Crown*, it was the nearest to welcome the river trade.

Benfleet's one-time importance as a wharf is underlined by a listing in the General Index of *The Overseas Trade of London Exchequer Customs Accounts 1480-81* (i.e. ships recorded in English customs documents). Among mentions of both English and Continental ports, the home port of the ship *Kateryn* was given as Benfleet.

King Henry VIII sailed for France on 14 July 1544 to join his troops. In September he captured Boulogne. He sailed on the *Katherine Pleasaunce*, one of the first ships of his new navy. The logistics of its construction give an excellent insight into the kind of activity Benfleet creek enjoyed. This royal ship had been built in Deptford from timber largely felled in the forest of Thundersley Park. William Cotyll received 13s. 9d. for the wages of labourers at 4d. and 6d. a day cutting wood. The wood was transported to Benfleet in 31 cart loads at fourpence each, from where 'Peter Collier of Benfleet' moved it in 14 loads to the shipyards in Deptford. He

was paid 14 shillings for his efforts. Under the terms of the Forest Law the actual timber would have belonged to the Crown. We can get some idea of what the *Katherine Pleasaunce* may have looked like; almost exactly a year later, on 19 July 1545, a similar ship, the *Mary Rose*, sank off Portsmouth in front of the king's eyes.

England's fledgling navy demanded from the port-towns a supply of armed merchantmen and other ships as a second line of defence to its men-of-war. A survey in 1564 recorded for South Benfleet five vessels, five masters and owners and 15 mariners and fishermen.

Thousands of wood loads were carried by water from South Benfleet to Westminster Abbey. In 1559 we learn of: 'Chardges for ffellyng, cuttyng, byndyng, warfage, cariage as well by Land and by Water of the Wood to Westminster ...' Another entry records some respectable sums of money for the time: '...for ffellyng, cutting and bindyng of 200 Lode of ffaggotts (bundles of sticks for fuel, but also as drainage base for road surfaces) £33. Warfage £20. Cariage by Water to Westminster £6.' (In April 1794, John Cowper, eldest son and heir of Nich. Cowper, farmer of South Benfleet, is mentioned as 'faggot-binder'.)

The 'hoy' is mentioned in Westminster accounts as early as the 16th century: 'Item to Mr Appleton's Watermen for going to sea to provide a Hoye – 12d.' It is said that in Benfleet almost every farmer had his own 'hoy' by the 18th century, a boat designed for carrying his produce up and down the river, like hay from Canvey to the cab horses of London, returning laden with their useful organic manure.

To the west of the *Hoy*, where Church Creek afforded access, the thatched buildings of the sawmill survived into the last century. A sea-food and cockle stall now lines the side of Church Creek. Across the road, next to the *Crown*, stood stables for the horses needed to haul the timber.

An old story, if true, tells how a Benfleet incident might have changed British history. According to Walter Bingham, who collected the story from old parish inhabitants and published it in the parish magazine in November 1937, two men had sought passage on board a boat in South Benfleet. This was in 1638, when the Star Chamber issued a decree forbidding ships to take emigrants from England to the American colony of New England. Thus prevented from sailing, the two men had to hire horses and a guide to London. The would-be emigrants are said to have been Oliver Cromwell and John Hampden.

In 1935 Benfleet was still a registered 'port', though little port business survived because of changing modes of transport.

Religious Upheavals

South Benfleet did not escape the religious and political changes of Henry VIII, Edward VI, Queen Mary and Queen Elizabeth I. In 1548, when an inquisition was ordered into the property of all churches in the kingdom, fearing seizure as with the monasteries, the Benfleet churchwardens 'sold of the Church Plate one

Chalice for 5 marks', which was used in part for church repairs, but also perhaps to do the right thing, 'partlie in setting for the Souldiers towards the Kinges majesties Wars …'.

Roger Appleton of Jarvis Hall is said to have been instrumental in bringing to trial William Tyms, deacon and curate of Hockley and Robert Drake, rector of Thundersley. They were subsequently burnt at the stake at Smithfield on 23 April 1556. Thomas Causton of Thundersley had been burnt at the stake at Rayleigh on 23 March 1555.

Benfleet's Thomas Wilson seems to have been an absentee for most of his ministry. Having survived the foundation of the Church of England and the changeover to Protestantism in the reign of Edward VI, he was now removed. A new vicar, Robert Bacon, arrived on 1 January 1555. Two vicars, John Holyman and Thomas Parker, followed in quick succession. Mary's reign ended with her death in November 1558. The following year the elusive Thomas Wilson was reinstated to his living in Benfleet. His death

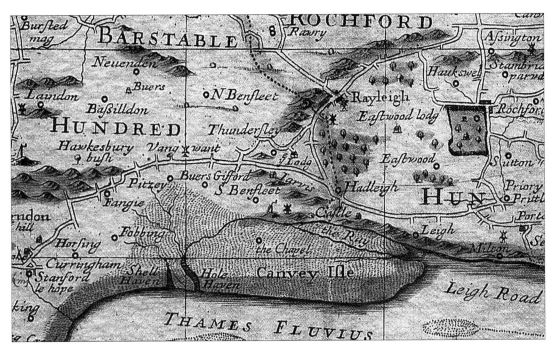

27 Ogilby and Morgan's map of 1678. Note the beacon and windmill on the Downs at today's St Mary's Road.

followed only a few months later and he was succeeded by a puritan, John Garrett.

The new vicar in 1562, John Garrett, was a reformer and refused to wear the surplice when taking a service. Henry Wood, churchwarden and local farmer of some substance, tried to compel him. An entry in the Registers of the Archdeacon's Court elaborates the story: 'A.D. 1566. Against the Vicar, because he will not minister in a surplice, and came to the house of Henry Wood with his bow and arrows, to seke for the said Wood.' God's not so holy representative vicar Garrett was 'tried, fined and dismissed'.

In 1582 the village clerk John Malvill was taken to court for preaching 'an extreme Puritan sermon'.

The village green was the scene of a disturbance on the Sunday before Michaelmas in 1597 by one William Haynes, who was brought before the ecclesiastical court 'detected for dancing with Minstrells on a green during afternoon service'.

Nor did Benfleet escape the accusations of witchcraft. In 1599 John Watson and 'Mrs' Watson of South Benfleet were accused of being or consorting with witches.

Another non-resident minister was John Grant from 1586 to 1609. His successor, John Bailey, was similarly absent: '1612. A Complaint against Master Bailey the Vicar, for that he is not resident, insomuch that sometimes for a whole month together there is nobody to bury the dead, nor to christen.' The churchwarden had turned to the Archdeacon's Court, which found that Bailey, too, had to resign.

Under Queen Elizabeth religious intolerance became treason; non-attendance at the parish church meant trial at Quarter Sessions rather than at the Archdeacon's Court: '1622. Ann Bruer, Singlewoman, for not being in Church for three Months.'

South Benfleet's church itself fell into serious disrepair during that period. Officers of the diocese, visiting in 1616, reported: 'Sir Edward

Bullock Kt, for not repayring the Chancell which is a great Annoyance to the Church ...'

John Evans was vicar 1688-95.

In 1689-90 village gossip would have been dominated by the case of the stolen bells at neighbouring Hadleigh. Jonathan Clarke of South Benfleet, victualler, had been indicted at Essex Quarter Sessions in January 1690, because with others he 'took and carried away two bells worth £60, belonging to the parishioners of Hadleigh in the custody of the churchwardens'. Clarke must have been a strong lad – the weight of the bells totalled about 12 cwt. His accomplices – Thomas Joce, a blacksmith, and John James, a farmer – both of Hadleigh, were accused of attempting to bribe witnesses to the tune of £5 to deny what they overheard at the *Boares Head Inn* (now the *Castle*), where seemingly they boasted about their achievements. Curiously, in 1691 a Jonathan Clarke and Tho. Banbury, the Benfleet blacksmith, acted as overseers of the poor. They were reselected the following year. Hadleigh's church of St James the Less only owns one bell today.

The Beacon on the Downs

John Ogilby and William Morgan's map of 1678 (as also later maps) features a post mill on the ridge of the South Downs, which is now remembered in Mill Hill, St Mary's Road. To the west of it, on the edge of the high ground, stood a beacon which was part of a line of signal stations that could be lit as warning of enemy sightings at sea. They lined the Essex coast from Harwich, via Walton's Naze, Point Clear near St Osyth and Foulness (and even out on sandbanks such as 'Whittaker' and 'Shooe' Beacons) to the east and on towards London via Langdon Hills and what is now Purfleet. Inland, the beacon trail ran via Beacon End near Colchester and Beacon Hill near Great Totham. Many other beacons are remembered in street names.

IV

The Seat of the Appletons

Sweyne Properties

Even before the Conquest of 1066 and since, the powerful Sweyne (Swein) had owned land in East Anglia. William I increased his holdings and his seat became Rayleigh castle. His son Robert, known as fitzSweyne, married Gunnora, daughter of Roger Bigod. (His second wife was Alice, daughter of Aubrey de Vere of Castle Hedingham.) Robert's son by Gunnora was Henry fitzRobert, better known as Henry of Essex. A favourite of the young King Henry II, he was 'Staller' or Standard Bearer, as former Wimarcs had been.

In 1157 the young king was ambushed by the Welsh at Cynesyllt. During the confusion Henry of Essex is said to have shouted 'The King is dead!' and run away. He survived that, but six years later, during a dispute with Robert de Montford, Earl of Leicester, he was accused of cowardice. This had to be resolved by trial by combat – a duel without body armour and carrying only a small shield of leather and a stave tipped with horn. God would be the judge. Henry was struck down, but, thought to be dying, he was spared by the king and his body was handed over to the monks of Reading. He lived, but his lands were lost and he spent the rest of his days as a landless monk, ending one of the most powerful dynasties in 12th-century England.

Following Henry de Essex, owners of this estate were the de Woodhams, according to the historian Philip Morant. They were succeeded by John de Coggeshall. Of William de Coggeshall's

four daughters Alice, the second, married Sir John Tyrell of Herons. Joyce, daughter of Sir Robert Tyrell, brought the estate to Thomas Appleton of Suffolk in marriage. Their son became Sir Roger Appleton of 'Bemflet'.

Three generations later, Henry Appleton held 'a mansion house called Northmayes, alias Jarvis Hill'.

Sir Roger Appleton, following his father Roger, died in 1557.

The Appletons were a distinguished and wealthy family. Three of them, Sir Henry (Knight), Roger (M.D.) and William (LL.D. – Dr of Laws), purchased an exemption from the Forest Law in 1563. Under the agreement, referred to as the Disafforestation, the Crown gave up its rights – for a not insubstantial consideration of £500 – over all the people living there. However, large-scale felling of trees would not be commencing.

Ever since Henry de Essex, following his 'Trial by Battle' under King Henry II in the 12th century, had lost all the possessions of the House of Wimarc to the Crown, the manors of Rayleigh with Hadleigh, Thundersley and Eastwood had been part of the Royal Forest. It spelled misery for the people living there. The Norman kings' fondness for hunting meant that the Law of the Forest was applied. To the Normans the life of a deer or a dog was worth more than the life of a common man. Trespassers, poachers and those who slew deer could expect punishment, which included lopping off fingers and hands, blinding or even death. Now, thanks to the

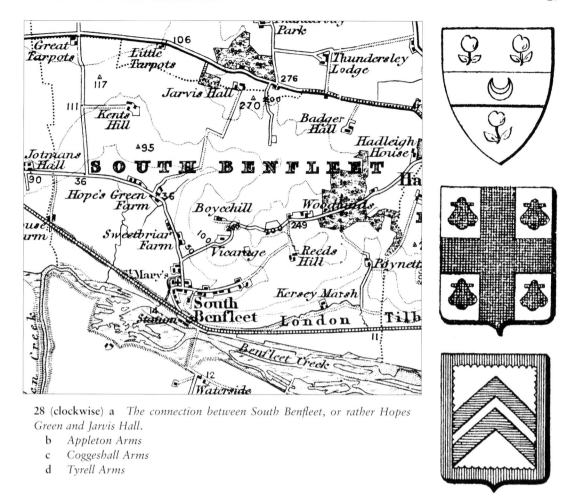

28 (clockwise) a *The connection between South Benfleet, or rather Hopes Green and Jarvis Hall.*
  b   *Appleton Arms*
  c   *Coggeshall Arms*
  d   *Tyrell Arms*

Appletons, the villagers would no longer pay fines and dues to the Queen, only to the lord of the manor.

The document of release names much more than the four parks in and around Benfleet. There are woods, wicks, marshes and feedings, including: 'The Manor of Jarvis-Hall (containing 6660 acres), Jarvis Hall Park, North Moyes Park, South Bemflet Park, Jarvis Great Woods, Jarvis High Woods, Jarvis Springs, Thundersley Great Woods, Hadleigh Great Woods, Dawes Woods, Dawes Heath, Hopes Green, Reeds Hills, Boyses, North, South, East and West Downs with divers marshes on Canvey Island (containing 3800 acres), the Wicks and Manor of South Bemflet (containing some 3000 acres).' Also the farm of Leigh-Park. It takes in

land as far as Hole Haven, which at that time was part of South Benfleet parish.

The complete list shows that timber-felling, fishing, oyster-farming and sheep-rearing were the main industries of the area.

In about 1564 Henry Appleton held four marshes or wicks of Sir William Petre (d. 1572) of Ingatestone Hall. The rent was payable in kind, and the list shows what could be taken from land and waterways annually and what might end up on the table: 60 three-year-old wethers (male castrated sheep) 'unshorne in their Woll' and 22 'good and sound Ewe Sheep in their Woll of two Yeres Age'. Also 'six good fresh Salmon of the largest Sorte'. More surprising to us today are 'Curlew', 'Teale', 'Plover', 'Mallard', 'Duck', 'Whinne', 'Hott',

'Snite', 'Redshankes' and 'Oxbirdes' (probably starlings).

In 1606 one 'Henry Appulton died in possession of the manor of Bemfleet Hall', which he had purchased from the Earl of Sussex and others and which he held under the Dean and Chapter of Westminster. Henry Appleton also held from the Dean and Chapter in South Benfleet a farm called Hollybones. Bullens and Reades (Reeds Hill) belonged to him, as well as a marsh in Hockley and various wicks and marshes in Canvey Island.

His son and heir Roger was 30 years old at his father's death. He was created a baronet on 29 June 1611, but died three years later. His

29 *Jarvis Hall today.*

30 *View from Jarvis Hill to the Water Tower,* c.1920.

succeeding son and grandson were both called Henry. The most famous of the Appletons was Sir Henry, Bart (1598-1648).

The Dean's Visits

Westminster Abbey leases describe the manor of South Benfleet as including 'the Rectory and Parsonage therewith, the Mansion House of the said Parsonage, all the Edifices, Lands, Tenements, Meadows, Pastures, Ffording Waters and Ffishing to the said Mannor belonging ...' The conditions of the leases contain directives to 'give and provide for the Dean, Treasurer, Steward, Surveyor and Receiver of the said Collegiate Church and all those coming with them or holding court there or to survey the said Mannor sufficient and good Hospitality of Meat, Drink and Lodging, Hay, Oates and Litter for their Horses ...'

Benfleet Hall Manor was leased from the Dean and Chapter of Westminster by the Appletons, which may explain the confusion of a third manor in Benfleet. It would also explain their involvement with Benfleet village and why, in 1576, the Dean spent time at the Appleton household on Jarvis Hill.

Today, many Benfleet inhabitants travel daily back and forth to London as commuters. The modes of transport in 1576 are interestingly detailed in the Dean of Westminster's expense account, which also give a particular insight into domestic arrangements of the time. The Dean's party arrived by river, first in two boats from Westminster Bridge to the *Old Swan* near London Bridge and then on by tilt boat to 'the Hard' at South Benfleet (Southebemflete) creek at a cost of 26 shillings and eightpence (26s. 8d.). A tilt boat was fitted with a 'tilt' or awning for the greater comfort of the passengers. The expense account for the trip even allows beer money for the watermen. (On another trip the Dean paid three pence at his lodgings to a boy for 'wipeynge myn Sheues' during his stay.)

When the Dean reviewed his list of personal expenses at the Appletons, he passed the one shilling and sixpence he had incurred when 'rowing on the water', but he personally crossed out the two shillings and fourpence (2s. 4d.) he'd lost at cards to 'Mrs Appulton' and altered the final total in his own hand. Was he ashamed to admit his gambling losses to the lady of the house?

He had officially handed three shillings to 'Mr Appultons two children and his brother Edward', two shillings to the 'Cooke and the Butteler', but three shillings and four pence 'unto the Serving Made'. The other maids shared a half crown between them.

Twilight of the Appletons

It was Sir Henry Appleton, the best known of that family, who, with seven others, sought out Dutch merchant entrepreneur Joas Kroppenburg in 1621 in order to embank Canvey Island at a fee of a third of the inned land, bringing in Dutch experts who left their mark on the island with their curious octagonal houses.

That same Sir Henry organised a body of men from South Benfleet and district to join King Charles I's army against the Scots in 1640. Though their destination was the border country, the 300 men only made it as far as Cambridge. There was such confusion and such poor organisation that the men, many of whom had been pressed into service, rebelled and eventually drifted back home in small groups.

During the Civil War Sir Henry Appleton, Cavalier, and his small contingent from the Rochford Hundred were lucky to escape with their lives when they were besieged in Colchester, together with other Royalist forces, by Roundheads under Fairfax from 13 June to 27 August 1648. Afterwards two-thirds of the Appleton lands were sequestrated. Sir Henry's death came within a few months of the surrender. He was buried at Great Baddow. (With Sir Henry at the Colchester siege was one William Land, who died in a foray outside one of the city gates, an ancestor of the Land family who would later be mine hosts at the *Anchor Inn* for generations.)

Even following the loss of two-thirds of the estate, Jarvis Hall land extended down to and across what is now the High Road. It was another Sir Henry Appleton who cancelled the village fair in 1665 to avoid the spreading of the plague.

Sir William Appleton (Bart) died on 15 November 1705, aged 77, followed by his lady Dorothy on 16 December 1719, aged 84.

---

31 *Jarvis Hall barn in April 1908, when 'this splendid site and old historical building' was offered for sale by T. Attwell of Benfleet.*

32 *In this view to Thundersley from Benfleet, the dilapidated barn that once was King John's Hunting Lodge can still be seen in its dominant position extreme left on the horizon (enlarged inset), next to the tall trees around Jarvis Hall.*

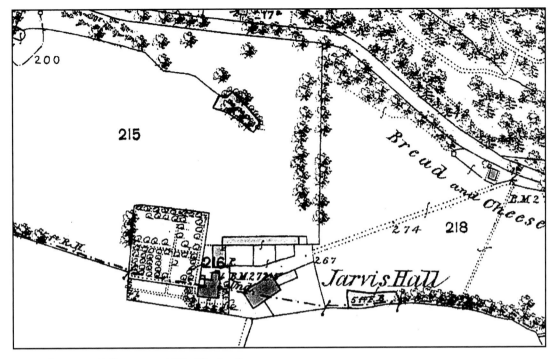

33(a) *The Jarvis Hall estate in 1838. The Benfleet-Thundersley parish border ran through the house and the barn.*

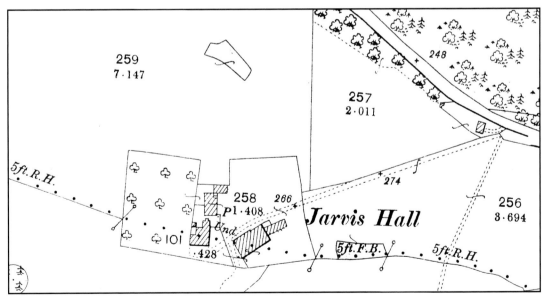

(b) *The division of 1896 separated the 'Hunting Lodge' barn from the main house. The oddly angled extension to the east is still the base of an outhouse.*

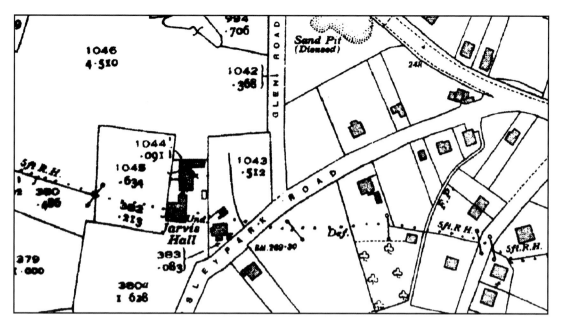

(c) *The private house was built in 1920. By 1939 Thundersley Park Road and Glen Road had been added. They are still unmade.*

Their three sons William, John and Henry died without issue. The two elder sons, William and John, together with their parents, rest under the chancel floor of South Benfleet church. An inscription seems to foresee the demise of the family name:

'Two Blooming Youths, Can you Forbeare a Groane
Inclosed, ly Beneath this Marble Stone!'

For over 200 years, following the Woodhams in the 13th century and the Coggeshalls in the 14th, the Appletons had remained at Jarvis Hall until Sir Henry Appleton, last of the brothers, died in 1708.

The inheritance came to the sister, Elizabeth Appleton, who in 1710 'brought the estates of the Manors of South Benfleet and Jarvis to her husband Richard Vaughan of Shenfield in marriage' and then to their son John. The Appletons had come by the estate in similar fashion, when Joyce, a daughter of Sir Robert Tyrell, married Thomas Appleton. The wheel had turned full circle ...

Changes of Fortune on Jarvis Hill

Unlike the Appletons, the Vaughans were absentee landlords. They had owned Shenfield Place for some time and it seems that Jarvis Hall was leased out. Elizabeth Vaughan, née Appleton, gave birth to five children – William (who died young), John, Stephen, Sophia and Jane. John married Ellen, the daughter of Nicholas Partridge of Doddinghurst. They had a son, Richard. John Vaughan, aged 40 in 1734, held estate estimated at £500 according to the Essex Freeholders Book of that year. He is mentioned mainly in Shenfield registers and died in 1765. Owner of a considerable fortune, Charles Richard Vaughan, 'an infant', is shown in the court roll of 1769 as the lord of the manor. In 1774 he is recorded in a deed as Richard Vaughan of Golden Grove in the county of Carmarthen. He died in 1786.

John Vaughan sold Jarvis Hall estate, as well as Hopes Green Farm, Curds Farm, Mucking Farm, Gravel Pit Farm and 'a very desirable Estate called Shenfield Place' on 8 February 1787 by auction (at Garraway's Coffee House,

Change Alley, London) for £8,310. The 'late' Charles Richard Vaughan is mentioned. The tenant of Hopes Green Farm at that time was Robert Loten, the Benfleet hoyman who left the bread charity to the poor of the parish.

Jarvis Hall was sold for £1,700 and Hopes Green Farm for £1,030. Priestley found that, according to the Manor Rolls, 'Swan Tabrum became Lord of the Manor by purchase before the Court met in 1787', which agrees with the auction date in February that year. In 1799 Swan (Samuel) Tabrum had a hand in enclosing part of Hopes Green, which was disputed by South Benfleet Manor, though no action seems to have been taken.

According to Benton, whose *History of Rochford Hundred* was published in 1867, Swan Tabrum disposed of the seat of the Appletons to Abraham Bullen in 1806, who resold it to the Perrys of Moor Hall, Harlow.

The boundary between South Benfleet and Thundersley parishes passed right through the Elizabethan house, as well as through the large barn next door, the reputed site of one of King John's hunting lodges.

On 6 September 1890 the 225 acres of Jarvis Hall and Hopes Green Farm were auctioned as 'valuable freehold estate' at the *Royal Hotel*, Southend. Jarvis Hall was described as 'pleasantly situated on high and park-like ground …' and thought to be a great acquisition 'to a City man fond of wild fowling'. The house, stables and barns are described, as well as a dairy and a brewhouse. The 'large productive garden' was 'well stocked with fruit trees'.

A small, unassuming enamel plaque marks the gate that leads to Jarvis Hall today, a family home in large grounds, where an unadopted section of Thundersley Park Road falls away steeply from the escarpment which continues through Bread and Cheese Hill and affords sweeping views from Thundersley church.

Some of the remarkable beams in the surviving barns and outhouses are thought to come from the original house. The property has been divided. In 1920 the dilapidated remains of the large barn, with its royal hunting lodge past and magnificent views, were replaced by a modern home. There is still an outhouse whose lower sections retain the thick moulded brick wall of a much earlier building. It stands at an odd angle to the house and is shown as an extension to the barn on old maps.

V

Vestry Meetings and Village Life

In the 16th century the parishes, with their elected, but unpaid, local representatives headed by the churchwardens, had to answer to the Justices of the Peace in Quarter Sessions.

Vestry meetings became an integral part of village life, when the community of farmers, hoymen (bargees), sawyers, wheelwrights, carpenters, horse-handlers, faggot binders, shopkeepers, innkeepers, and others met annually to run village affairs, the minutiae of local government. The clerk took notes, the vicar or, more usually, a curate was present, and the village elders would appoint the people to run their affairs for the coming year – the churchwarden, someone to look after the poor, someone to ensure that the roads were passable, and finally one or two constables.

Constables were younger men as a rule, where brawn was needed; some of them later took over other offices. They, in turn, had to report annually to a travelling court of High Constables, and we have several reports of the Benfleet constables' attendance.

One of the functions of the churchwarden was to pay village expenses, for example, when the bells had to be rung in relays from dawn to dusk, as noted by John Lowry on 5 August 1713: '… paid for Ringing ye Quens Crownation Day – 5 shillings; … for Ringing when ye Peace was proclaimed – 10 shillings; … for Ringing ye Thanks giving Day – 5 shillings.' Other holidays were Gunpowder Plot on 5 November and Christmas Day on 25 December. The

anniversary of Queen Anne's coronation had been on 23 April.

From 1701 to 1713 England, as part of the Grand Alliance, had fought France and Spain in the War of Spanish Succession. The Duke of Marlborough triumphed in many battles and in 1704 the British fleet under Sir George Rooke captured Gibraltar. In April 1713 England made peace with France and, two months later, with Spain. On the general proclamation of peace, as all over England, Benfleet parish celebrated with a holiday and more bell ringing than usual. The churchwarden's ten shillings would have supplied 60 quarts of good ale or 120 of small beer and must have kept the whole population of the parish merry.

Churchwarden's obligations and 'Noysome Fowles and Vermin'

As if life was not difficult enough for humans to keep their heads, Queen Elizabeth's 'Act for the Preservation of Grayne from Noysome Fowles and Vermin' authorised churchwardens to pay set fees to anyone who could prove to have eliminated small animals and birds. The heads would do as proof: heron and osprey heads were valued at four pence. Old crows, choughs, rooks were three pence. Merlins, hawks, kites, buzzards, shags, cormorants two pence. Kingfishers were one penny, as were six young crows, six unbroken eggs and 12 sparrows' heads. Polecats, weasels, stoats and wildcats earned one penny. The heads of otters and hedgehogs brought two pence. Moles were worth only a halfpenny and every three rats and 12 mice were valued at a penny.

According to Benfleet Parish Accounts, even in 1712-13 churchwarden John Lowry paid out two shillings for a fox and a badger, five shillings for five foxes, two shillings for two badgers ... among others. As such skins were often nailed to the church door, possibly as proof in the absence of the warden, in many villages stories arose that human skin had been found under old nails, as happened in Benfleet, too.

A Vestry Meeting at the *Crown*

On Easter Tuesday 1732 the parish clerk recorded an exception from meeting in the Vestry. With a flourish and in a fine hand, filling a page in the Accounts Book, he began with the admission: 'At a Vestry of all the Parishioners of South Benfleet held by an Adjournment from the parochial church to the *Crown* ...' The *Crown Inn's* warm and welcoming hearth may have been the more popular option for conducting village business.

The venue of that Vestry meeting in 1732 was today's *Half Crown*. It may have started as a Customs and Excise post before it became a public house, and by 1792 it was referred to as a butcher's shop.

Thomas Barber, apothecary/surgeon of South Benfleet, owned two tenements in Kent, three in Rayleigh and one house at Church Gate, South Benfleet, apart from his own. In his last will and testament in 1762 Barber left everything to his wife Elizabeth for her lifetime, after which it would pass on to Catherine, wife of Robert Hanson (a farmer of nearby Vange), to be equally divided amongst 'the heirs of her body lawfully to be begotten'.

(Thomas Barber attended parish Vestry meetings from 1734 until 1749, serving occasionally as constable or overseer of the poor. Thomas Hanson served a similar time-span to Thomas Barber − 1735 until 1752 − acting as overseer of the poor and churchwarden.

In 1734 Thomas Hanson married Susannah Vandevord at Hadleigh and in 1749 one of the same name married Jane Greenaway on Canvey Island. Thomas Hanson held Canvey's Waterside Farm.)

Almost 27 years after Thomas Barber's will, one of Catherine Hanson's four children, 'Robert Hanson, Rochester, now Shenfield, Essex, Saddler and Collarmaker, Gentleman', sold his quarter share of the inheritance by deed document for five shillings. In that document he recited the properties again, but itemised one house in Benfleet in particular, the *Crown*, which 'used to be a pub, now a private house together with butcher's shop, slaughter house, stable, yards, gardens, orchards and wharfs'.

The gravestone of 'Catherine Henson [*sic*] wife of Robert Henson', though weathered, can still be found in Benfleet's churchyard. One of the old shops opposite the church in the High Street still carries the name Hanson.

Benfleet Ladies

In one sense South Benfleet was ahead of its time, perhaps because of the unavailability of suitable or willing male officers. In 1744 both the overseers of the workhouse near the churchyard, an establishment Benfleet shared with Thundersley, were female. Replacing John Fitch in parish matters, Mrs Fitch became overseer of the poor in 1744, sharing that position with Heather Jeniens (Jenkins) and in 1745 and '46 she was joint overseer with male parishioners. Ann Brewett (Brewitt) and Susanna Grenaway (Greenaway) jointly served in 1751. In 1759 and again in 1771 Mrs Ann Brewitt held the office. The only woman's signature in the vestry minutes appears in 1758 − that of Susan Greenaway as surveyor of highways. Mrs Hollex held that office in 1775 and Ann Brewitt in 1779. Only in 1788 did the law confirm 'that a woman was eligible for the office of Parish Overseer.'

Members of these families are buried locally. A John Greenaway of Canvey Island and Johanna Greenaway rest under an almost illegible gravestone in Benfleet's churchyard. Haggar Greenaway was landlord at the *World's End* – now the *Lobster Smack* tavern – on Canvey Island in 1770.

It was unusual in the past for women to have ownership, but when Mary, 'widow and executrix of John James of Canvey Island', married Thomas Spittey of Rettendon, who was described as 'gentleman', she nevertheless spelled out her ownerships in a pre-nuptial arrangement, listing what she'd inherited from her father Lawrence Skylder, what she had 'subsequently purchased', and in which she had right of dower as widow of John James.

In most cases, however, women did not reach such lofty heights. The historian Philip Benton mentions an indenture from the Benfleet parish chest which indicates that it was usual in Queen Anne's reign to place girls as apprentices for a term of years, 'to learn the business of housewifery'.

Poignant stories underline the prevailing attitudes of earlier times, as when 'Edward, the base born child of Prudence Couch' was laid to rest. At Epiphany Court Session in 1698 Joseph Evans of Canvey Island – 'insula de Canvy' – was summoned by John Smager, John Skilder, Peter Bell and Moses Eliams to answer the overseers of South Benfleet for 'getting Mary Wapoole with child of a bastard'.

Local records of that time tell of 'stranger men' being buried and 'travelling women' dying in the poorhouse. In 1690, when John Evans was vicar, James Purckes (Purkiss) made an agreement with the parish, to pay '... for the Smith's shop belonging to the poor annually one pound and keep it in good repair'. That rent was mentioned again in 1700. The earliest record was in 1684, when John Carter was blacksmith and promised to 'pay yearly and every Yeare during his occupying ye said Shopp the Sume of Twentie Shillings of lawful Money of England unto ye Overseer of ye Poore ...'

Between the *Hoy* public house and the churchyard wall, the smithy survived well into the last century. In 1908 H. Clark advertised as 'General Smith, Farrier and Ironmonger, Agricultural and Domestic Machinist', with merchandise that ranged from roofing felt to shovels.

Benfleet's Tithes

Benton tells us that the (original?) site of the vicarage was in a croft of about a rood (the fourth part of an acre), called 'the heart', adjoining the church wall on the north side. A house stood there in 1610, when the north entrance to the church would have offered convenient access.

In June 1711 the Rev. Henry Compton, Bishop of London from 1674 to 1713, visited Benfleet at the behest of the influential vicar, Edward Roberts, A.M. (1704-18), who served the village by horse from Rayleigh, where he was rector. The Bishop pronounced the site of the vicarage unfit and 'prevailed upon Westminster to provide a new piece of Ground to build a House upon'.

The Rev. Roberts had come to Benfleet from Grimsby and he knew his rights. On 4 December 1706 he noted for the benefit of his successors: '...The vicarage is endowed with all Manner of Tithe whatsoever except the corn which belongs to the Patrons the Dean and Chapter of Westminster. So all along paid beyond memory.'

The tithes included hay, wool, lamb, calves, milk, among other things. 'And when the Tithe is paid in kind, each Inhabitant is bound to bring Milk every tenth day both Morning and Evening to the Church Porch ... and to pay the 10th Calf, the 10th Lamb, the 10th Fleece or in Proportion.'

That wasn't all. 'Item, each House or Cottage in the Parish pays by Custom from Time immemorial 2 shillings in the £ Rent to the Vicar by two even half-yearly Payments, that is to say Lady Day and Michaelmas, this indeed is a modus and amounts to about £6 per annum.' And so on ... this statement covers 60 households in 1706.

34 *View from creekside early in the 1920s. The various buildings that make up the* Hoy *dominate the centre right, with the sawmill buildings to the left. Weatherboarded 'Wharf House', front right, was said to have been built on two barges.*

35 *'The old Parlour', Hoy Inn, 1914-15, much as it is today.*

Customs and Excise

With its proximity to the Thames, Benfleet did not escape the attention of the Customs and Excise men, when smuggling was a way of life for so many. The Customs Service was set up on a national basis in 1671. In Benfleet its likely base was the *Crown*, before that became a public house in the 18th century.

Of three riding officers who patrolled the coast on horseback – a dangerous occupation rewarded with a substantial £50 p.a. each – one Isaac Harrison came from South Benfleet in 1765. Was it the same Isaac Harrison who became overseer of the poor that very year? Edward R. Harris, Officer of Excise, was present at the induction into the vicarage of the Rev. Edward Roberts in May 1704, as were John Lowry, churchwarden and James Lord, parish clerk.

In his *History of Canvey* (1902), A.L. Daly relates how, at a house on Canvey Island owned by farmer Jan Smagge (John Smager?), ghostly hauntings and eerie groans and screams drew people from near and far to witness the events while the smugglers arrived with contraband. Otherwise conflicting reports place the happenings precisely on 10, 13, 14 and 16 September 1709, when spirits were exorcised, it transpires, by the Benfleet parish clerk, James Lord.

H.E. Priestley and Wyn T. Phillips, in their *History of Benfleet, Book Two*, found smuggling activities in Benfleet's waterways from records kept in the Custom House in Maldon: '1733. Mr Vaughan (Lord of the Manor of Jarvis Hall) has

36 *The* Crown *in earlier days, but the picket fence had gone already.*

claimed as wreck some casks of spirits found sunk at Benfleet Creek. The Collector states that the goods were found by Customs Officers in a rill leading to the Creek. The casks were filled with spirits and secured to stakes so as not to float out at high water, therefore they are contraband and not wreck. At the time of the discovery the officers saw at a distance a boat with five men in her, two of whom are believed to have been Layzell and Gardner, notorious smugglers.'

Benfleet's five hostelries, the *Blue Anchor*, the *Hoy*, the *Crown* and two others listed in 1770, the *Chequer* and the *World's End* – the latter on Canvey Island – would likely have benefited from such illegal trade. Local legends insist that the church has at times doubled as a store house for many a half-anker or hogshead and the unproven tale of an underground tunnel from *Hoy* to the church still excites memories today.

The *Crown* was completely rebuilt in brick in the 19th century, though its name was changed to the *Half Crown* more recently. In 1969 a lorry demolished part of the building

and tongue-in-cheek regulars democratically voted for the change in its name.

On parish land behind the village, close to or on the site of the present car park, South Benfleet's cage with whipping post and stocks would hold offenders taken by the constables until they could be brought before the Justices.

By 1700 the population of the parish amounted to some 280 souls.

The 'Honest' Hoyman

James Mathews' gravestone epitaph, reported by Benton to be found in Benfleet's churchyard, gives perhaps a good idea of the lusty, good-humoured, hard-working community:

> Sixty-three years our hoyman sail'd merrily round,
> Fourty-four liv'd parishioner where he's Aground,
> Five wife's bear him thirty-three children Enough;
> Land another as honest before he gets off.

Apart from hoyman, Mathews (also Matthews) had at some time been overseer of the poor, surveyor of highways and churchwarden. He had arrived in the parish in 1684 and lived at Suttons farm. Astonishingly, the arms on his churchyard monument were 'Or, a stork close' (a stork, standing, wings closed, on a gold or yellow background). An unusual attribute, one would think, for a hoyman and farmer.

James Mathews served as overseer as early as 1697. In some years he appears to have been referred to as John. Whichever, he was still churchwarden at his death on 4 July 1728, aged 73 years. At the Easter Vestry meeting the following year his executors 'gave in their accounts ...' on his behalf.

James (or John?) Mathews had been recorded in 1712 and 1713 by the then churchwarden John Lowry as receiving payment for 'water caridge', supplying half a dozen 'Dall' (dale – the hollowed-out tree trunks for transporting water) for nine shillings and even earning the odd shilling for bringing in a fox or a badger, which were still pursued as vermin, together with many small creatures and birds since the act of Preservation of Grain in the eighth year of Queen Elizabeth I's reign.

From 1730 Mathews' vacant seat was taken by William Mathews, probably his son, who for over twenty years sat in on Vestry meetings, serving as overseer and churchwarden.

Brother of 'the Governor'

Another one-time 'hoyman' and yeoman of South Benfleet was Robert Loten, brother of the illustrious John Gideon Loten, known as Governor Loten, who made his name in India and England and who died at Utrecht in 1789, at 80 years of age. His memorial can be found in Westminster Abbey. The family originally came from Flanders.

Robert Loten, son of Robert, hoyman and yeoman, held Waterside Farm in Canvey at one time (which was formerly held by Thomas Hanson) and Hopes Green in Benfleet. His first wife was Sarah Greenaway, whom he married in Canvey Island chapel in 1750. Mary Marsh, widow of Rayleigh, followed c.1785. He died in Rayleigh on 10 May 1791. If we assume a similar age within a few years to the brother who is remembered in Westminster Abbey, he, too, must have been in his 80s on his death, which makes his second marriage six years earlier all the more remarkable. He had been a leading vestryman, twice churchwarden, twice overseer of the poor.

In 1774 Robert Loten was authorised, together with his brother-in-law John Greenaway, in a deed by 'Richard Vaughan, Lord of the manor of South Bemfleet, to take and keep for his [the lord's] use all wrecks of ships, vessels, boats, merchandises, or anything he could claim, within the boundary and limits of the said manor'. When Jarvis Hall was sold, in 1787, Robert Loten was listed as a tenant. (In 1807 Robert Loten was named as having enclosed parts of Hopes Green.)

In his will he appointed the south porch of Rayleigh church for distribution of the charities he founded, one of which was to hand out bread to the poor of South Benfleet parish.

Bells and Brewitts and Other Folk

Among the more prominent families of the times were the Bells of Thundersley Lodge, whose simple tomb can still be found in Benfleet churchyard. In 1655 one of the elders of the original Dutch timber chapel on Canvey Island was one Gilles Van Belle.

After the Restoration (1662-89) the Hearth Tax or Chimney Money was introduced. At that time the Bell family had nine hearths – more than any other in South Benfleet. A Giles Bell owned extensive lands in South Benfleet as well as 'hoys and other craft, ferrying cargoes up and down the river'.

In 1705 Peter van Bell together with others is mentioned in connection with outbuildings and both fresh and saltmarsh in Prittlewell and South Benfleet, which were probably the detached parts of those parishes in Canvey Island.

The Essex Freeholders Book of 1734 names Giles Bell of Thundersley Lodge, then aged 42, with an estimated £10 estate (though some aspects of that document seem to be based on guesswork). The family tomb marks his death on 28 November 1741, aged 55. His wife Joanna died in 1743, at 50 years of age. A daughter Mary Bell, aged 22, had been laid to rest in 1736. Giles Bell served as overseer of the poor in the early 1720s, but was succeeded by Lewis Bell in 1733 and in 1738 and 1743 by John Bell.

Jonas Asplin, doctor of Prittlewell, wrote in his diary on 18 May 1826: 'The report of the day is that Lieut. Eikin, who married Giles Bell's widdow, committed suicide in the King's Bench and that his family are on Thundersly parish, where he hired a large, poor, heavy land, farm.'

Neighbours in the churchyard are the Brewitts. John Brewitt senior died in 1749 while serving as churchwarden, aged 57. His first wife Mary had died 29 years earlier, his mother in 1729.

In 1737 the 43-year-old merchant John Brewett resided in South Benfleet with his second wife Anne and his son John. Ann lived until 1779, surviving son John by 20 years. John Brewitt was farmer and publican at the *Blue Anchor*. He had two sons, Henry and John and a daughter Elizabeth. John Brewitt (also Brewett) junior took up his parish duties as overseer of the poor the year after his father's death. He died in 1759. In 1770 Ann Brewitt was named as licensee of the *Blue Anchor*. Henry Brewett, grocer, son of John Brewitt, is mentioned by Benton as the name on one of Benfleet's 'peal of five bells', made in London in 1790. (There are six bells today.) He leased out his and Robert Loten's wharfs in a document of 1795 for £147.

According to the Essex Freeholders Book, Samuel James, who attended Vestry meetings mostly as churchwarden, was aged 22 at the time of publication (1734) and owned estate worth £10, while James Hickweed (also Hickwood or Kickweed), aged 50, had estate of £12. Perhaps the same, a James Kickweed, South Benfleet butcher, was accused in 1707 of 'keeping false Weights'.

The young Peter Smith, at 22, held a £60 farm: Tarpots. He replaced his churchwarden father as overseer in 1734 until 1739.

Daniel Bilt signed the Parish Accounts Book from 1737 to 1751, Isiah Harrington from 1739 to 1748 and Stephen Huntly left his mark from 1737 to at least 1752. Robt. Carpenter, a wheelwright, started serving as constable in 1734 and bowed out in 1749, having been overseer and churchwarden along the way. James Fford was a regular at Vestry meetings from 1726 to the last pages of the surviving Accounts Book in 1752. Joseph Deale (or Deals) served as constable from 1745 to 1748.

At the beginning of the 21st century, the phone book for the Southend area, under 'residential listings', holds an astonishing record of how many of these old names have survived in the area. There are 26 Appletons, 35 Vaughans, 133 Bells, but only two Brewitts.

Thirteen Greenaways stood the test of time. As for Mathews and Matthews, there are 168.

The Farming Community

In his *History of the Rochford Hundred* Philip Benton (1867-88) lists the main farms or estates in South Benfleet at the time: Little Tarpots, Badger Hall, Reeds Hill, Suttons, Hadleigh Cross, the old Manor Hall, Kents Hill Farm, Sweet Briar Farm, Hopes Green, Boyces, Hadleigh House and Great Tarpots are all mentioned.

Reeds Hill Farm is still operating as a farm today. The name refers back to William le Rede in 1285. Reeds Hills are listed in the Appleton document of the exemption from the Forest Law in Elizabethan time and again as belonging to the Appletons in 1606 as 'Reades' and in 1646 as 'Reads', when it was occupied by Thomas Whittop. The farm was probably among the lands Sir Henry lost following the siege of Colchester in 1648.

Reeds (Reads) Farm was 150 acres 'or thereabouts', of arable, meadow and pasture land when it was bought by John Nash in June 1791. In October 1861 Mrs Caroline Porter, the outgoing tenant, listed among the contents five cart horses, one short horned cow, one goat, 85 ewes and eight lambs, a brewhouse, fields, and more. The estimated value of the property was £500 15s. 5d. (The half-year vicarial tithe in January 1862 due to the vicar, T. Julius Henderson, was £12 1s. 2d.)

Reeds Hill was sold by John Nash of Inglesham, Faringdon, Berks. on 30 April 1863 to Joseph Augustus Browne, Gentleman, of Reeds Hill Farm, South Benfleet – Browne, who was born in Minchinhampton, Gloucestershire, had rented it for a year previously. Philip Benton commented: 'At Reed's Hill there is some good mixed soil'.

In the 1871 Census the 44-year-old J.A. Browne is recorded as being 'a farmer of 150 acres employing 6 men and one boy'. His Prittlewell-born wife Emma was 43. They had a three-year-old son, William Augustus, born

37   Mr Burton of Reeds Hill Farm with shire horses in 1908, on or just in front of what is now Essex Way. The only house, top left in the picture, is 'Highfields' on Vicarage Hill, which to date has had four owners: Brown, Martin, Preston and Smith.

at Reeds Hill. At this time the Brownes had four servants – William Livermore of South Benfleet, 13-year-old Elizabeth Cranfield from Leigh, and George and Mary Brewer, husband and wife.

Ten years later, besides Browne and wife, an 18-year-old daughter Annie is mentioned, plus a servant and a gardener. He now employed two boys as well as the six men.

By 1891 J.A. Browne, 'Farmer', was living at Reeds Hill Farm with just his son William and Annie Chandler, servant/general domestic, aged 27 years.

In November 1898 Rochford Rural District Council bought land for the water tower at £25 with a frontage of 75 feet. By 1905 Browne received letters from prospective purchasers asking for specific plots of land.

J.A. Browne died at Reeds Hill on 25 March 1920, aged 93. He left a son William Augustus

(and three grandchildren) and daughter Anne Emma (spinster). His daughter was left stock in the London, Tilbury and Southend Railway among other shares, the lands went to his son. And there was a cottage for life, one of six (Brownes Cottages), to servant Annie Chandler, free of any costs.

Suttons Farm had been inherited on the death of Lawrence Holder in 1702 by Mary, wife of John James. In 1717, on the death of John James of Canvey Island, his widow remarried Thomas Spittey of Rettendon, gentleman. In a lease for 99 years (deed of trust) to James Matthews of South Benfleet, mariner, and John James of Bowers Gifford, yeoman, Suttons Farm is mentioned as 25 acres among other properties. It had been in the occupation of James Waller.

Mary Spitty, formerly Mary James, left it to her son Samuel in 1751. Samuel James died in 1774, leaving the farm in trust for his son to Reginald Heber, Withers Jennings and Thomas and Ambrose Spitty. They sold it to Henry Brewitt, grocer, in 1778, who in turn left it to his son, Henry jun. (who was admitted on paying a fine – a registration fee – of £39).

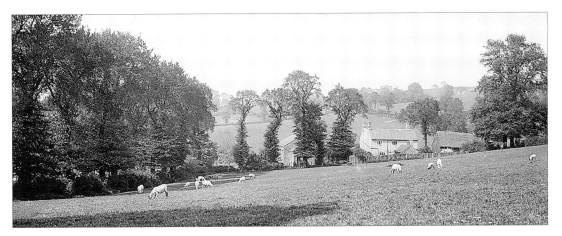

38 *A pastoral view of Benfleet in the early 1920s, across Endway and Vicarage Hill. School Lane runs behind the hedge to the left, and in the centre are the original Methodist church and Suttons farm. On the horizon, behind trees, we find Boyce Hill farmhouse.*

Henry Brewitt jun. mortgaged the property to 'Thomas Spitty of Billericay, Gent, and John Bailey, butcher of Gravesend', for £1,000. This was redeemed in July 1800 and the property sold to Daniel Nash, farmer. There followed two more generations of Nashes and other owners until in 1894 Henry Charles Long bought the whole property out of copyhold for £201 9s. 4d.

In spite of its position in South Benfleet, Hopes Green Farm used to be part of the Manor of Jarvis. For a while it became known as Little Jarvis. Tenant was Robert Loten when Jarvis Hall Manor was sold to Swan Tabrum in 1787. 'Hopes Green Farm in the Parish of South Benfleet containing 60 acres, let to Robert Loten at £12.' Its last building, a house called the Limes, survived into the last century at the bottom of Constitution Hill, on the site that is now the Benfleet Branch Library. Part of the farm used to be brick fields, about Sidwell Avenue, an area now covered in chalets.

Boyces has retained its name as Boyce Hill Golf Club. The high aspect of this area, too, is thought to have been the site of a mill once. It was Boyescroft in 1412 and a William Boyce

was recorded in 1563. In 1868 it was stated that the vicar had the right to use the well on Boyce Hill Farm at a charge of ten shillings per annum.

Jotmans Hall was associated with the family of James Jotman.

Shipwrights Wood was Shepewrightesfeld as long ago as 1315. Here the timber was prepared for boats that were built by the creek and elsewhere.

Tarpots had its name as early as 1405, when tar and pitch – produced by the distillation of wood – were needed for the caulking of boats. Great Tarpots was called Tarpodys in 1415 and Tarpottys in a document of 1424. By 1574 it was Tarpott. In the early 15th century the Attwood family held it in copyhold tenure. 30 acres lay in South Benfleet parish, plus Little Tarpots in Thundersley parish. Later it became 60 acres and Little Tarpots, including a neighbouring holding called Rushes, covered 37 acres. The two were joined in 1670, when Roger Reade owned them, though the Reades did not live at Tarpots. By 1723 it was in the ownership of Peter Smith, who served the parish as surveyor of highways in 1712 and as churchwarden from 1707 to 1711 and 1714 to 1723. Another Peter, probably his son, died young at the age of 23 in 1735.

About 1788, following several transactions, Tarpots Farm was bought by Thomas Spitty of Sadlers Farm, Bowers Gifford for £392 10s.,

40 Great Tarpots farm, c.1905. Now it is the site of a shopping arcade and petrol station.

41 The boundary between Benfleet and Thundersley parishes ran through Little Tarpots farm on the London Road (A13).

'who paid, at the request of Thomas Griffin to the Lord, all the principal moneys advanced to him.' Total cost of farm and appurtenances was £1,092 10s. The transfer 'fine' was £45 and the annual quitrent 10s. Spitty also bought Little Tarpots, paying a fine of £18 to the Lord of Jarvis Hall manor.

On his death in 1824 Thomas Spitty left his estates to his son, Captain Thomas Spitty of Billericay, and he in turn to his son Thomas Jenner Spitty, who died in 1898 without an heir. Eventually a widow Mary Anne Spitty and her solicitors claimed it. Ten years later it was inherited by Leonard Fothergill Carter of Crofton, Vancouver Island, Canada and nine years after that it was taken out of copyhold and became freehold land.

VI

Georgian Benfleet

Francis Clerke, 'Rector of North Benfleet'

To the north side of Benfleet's church of St Mary the Virgin, across a small brook and the tidal extremes of Church Creek, stood South Benfleet Hall. Then still owned by the Dean and Chapter of Westminster, Francis Clerke (Clark) was the lessee early in the 18th century. Clerke had also purchased a third of the right of presentation (advowson) to the rectory of Bowers Gifford. In his will he describes himself as 'Doctor of Laws, Rector of North Benfleete'. His second wife, Bridgett, whom he married in 1718 when she was 20 and he was 34, had died on New Year's Day 1730, at only 33 years of age. There were no children. Her death had left him devastated, as a sepulchral scroll on the chancel wall in St Mary's church testifies.

In the nave on the west wall of St Leonard's, Shoreditch in London, a draped marble tablet remembers Clerke's parents. His father, also a cleric by the name of Francis Clerke, was formerly rector of Stoke D'Abernon in Surrey, and his mother Sarah was 'the youngest child of Richard Banks, lapidary to three Kings'. They had married in London in 1671.

The tablet was erected by their 'grateful son', Francis, the youngest and only surviving of 14 brothers with one sister, Sarah, who were born in 19 years of marriage. Sarah survived Francis Clerke and inherited his estate. The father died 1690 at 65 years of age, the mother in 1709, aged 64 years.

Francis Clerke matriculated at Merton College Oxford on 10 October 1700, aged 16,

received his B.A. four years later, his M.A. in 1707, and his B & D.C.L. – Doctor of Laws – in 1713-4. Incorporated at Cambridge in 1733, he became Chancellor of the Diocese of Chichester and also Commissary of the Deaconry of Lewes. These positions were followed by Justice for the Quorum for the County of Essex.

He seems to have taken quite an active interest in North and South Benfleet; he was, for instance, the author of the doggerel on James Mathews' gravestone. Another proof of his humour was a six-stanza epitaph to his predecessor as rector of North Benfleet, the Reverend Joseph Hazwell, in North Benfleet church.

According to the South Benfleet Vestry Book, on 22 April 1717 'the Revd Dr Francis Clerke may if he pleases build a pew in the North Aisle of the Church behind the Door for the perpetual Use of the Tenant dwelling in South Benfleet Hall for the time being.'

On Easter Tuesday 1733 the influential Dr Clerke attended the yearly Vestry meeting of South Benfleet parish to choose the churchwarden, the overseer of the poor, the surveyor of highways and the constable for the coming year. His imposing signature dominates the Accounts Book page which records the event. The following Easter Tuesday 'The Rev. Dr Clerke' was listed as one of the overseers of the poor, his signature far less flamboyant.

Another meeting was called that same year on 26 December, following his death, to select new officers. John Hows, Thos. Barber, Samuel

Eland and John Brewet shared the offices. Others present were Peter Smith, Tho. Sayer, James Hickweed and Wm. Mathews. Thos. Biddell, LL.B. was the officiating curate.

Francis Clerke's Will

In his will Clerke left Bonvilles, his farm in North Benfleet, to his cousin Ann Bate of Stock, spinster, together with his 'yellow bed, chairs, looking glass, plate, watch, ruby ring set with a diamond, my own picture and that of the Duchess of Cleveland'.

South Benfleet farm Clerke left to his brother-in-law Joseph Mayer, described as 'Gentleman' in later documents. To his sister, Sarah Mayer, he bequeathed three houses in and about the City of London among other things, including his own residence in Hoxton Square, Shoreditch. He also charged his sister 'In Trust' to have the chancel laid out in marble and to buy and set up a new organ in the parish church of South Benfleet '… in two years after my decease' and also to pay yearly for ever an organist £30 'to play upon the same'. This organist, significantly, is to be chosen and appointed not by the Mayers, but by the 'President and Treasurers of the Corporation of the Sons of the Clergy for the time being forever, with the preference always to a clergyman's son'. Francis

42 *Francis Clerke's will.*

Clerke himself, of course, was the son of a clergyman.

A Mr Poole of London sent a letter, dated 28 October 1736 – two years later – which urged the parish to take steps towards getting the will carried out and asking if anything had been done towards acquiring an organ. The writer added that Mr Mayer was trying to pick up a second-hand chamber organ for about £20 or £30. The Mayers' residence was at New Place, Upminster, now a modern housing estate.

Francis Clerke died at 50 years of age on 31 October 1734, three days after making his will, which was then proved on 5 November in the court of 'Edmund, by divine right Bishop of London'. Lawyers moved swiftly and on 'Friday the 8th next', at the Court of Assistants of the Corporation of the Sons of the Clergy, the Clerke will was read out: 'The Court took the same into consideration and have agreed the said Trust.'

This Charity still exists. It was an important benevolent organisation in its day, with a charter from Charles II in 1678. The trustees administered estates and properties left to them in Trust, paid pensions to clergymen's widows, supplied money for the education of their children, arranged apprenticeships for their sons. Unfortunately, I found no further mention of the Clerke trust in the Charity's minutes, which are otherwise meticulously kept. But the Benfleet Organ Fund dated back to 1735.

Francis Clerke and his second wife lie buried near the altar, as the memorial plaque states. It's as though he intended to lie beside his wife in marble halls, listening to organ music. Mysteriously, the cartouche-of-arms on the Clerke memorial of St Leonard's, Shoreditch in London has been damaged and the arms selectively erased, just like the one in South Benfleet's church.

The Maestro of South Benfleet

It seems that some people can influence the lives of others even from beyond the grave. Francis Clerke, doctor of laws and rector of North

43   *Erfurt, Thuringia, 1760.*

Benfleet, might have been surprised at the results of his last will and testament, which brought a German musician, organist, harpsichordist, violinist and composer to his small riverside harbour-village and who raised the name of South Benfleet, for a time at least, among lovers of baroque music.

Clerke's wish, that the Corporation of the Sons of the Clergy should make the appointment of this organist and the proviso that preference should be given to a son of a clergyman, proved significant.

George Frederick Handel had serenaded Queen Anne when he first arrived on these shores and had known her successors George I and George II in their native Hannover. Some of his finest music was written for royal occasions. He also gave a yearly concert on behalf of the Clergymen's Charity in St Paul's Cathedral. So an approach to him for help by that Charity would seem a reasonable proposition.

Around the summer of 1737 Handel became ill with what is now believed to have been a mild stroke. He had no use in his right hand and by the autumn he travelled to Aachen in Germany to 'take the waters'. Invigorated and revitalised, he returned to London by 7 November and began composing again immediately. His new opera was *Faramondo*.

When *Faramondo* was produced by the composer at the King's Theatre, London, in

January 1738, a 'Mr Mantel' is named as one of the subscribers. That is the earliest known record of Benfleet's new organist Johann Christian Mantel in England and would place his arrival here around 1737.

Later Handel reciprocated by becoming a subscriber to Mantel's music.

Handel's home was in Halle, Saxony. One of Mantel's brothers was a medical doctor and brewer in Gotha, the home town of Handel's favourite niece and executrix.

My finding Mantel's last will and testament at the Public Record Office, London, in the Prerogative Court of Canterbury division, has only recently opened up the life of the organist and composer, as it revealed his original name – Johann Christian Scheidemantel. (A PCC will represents people of high standing, whose affairs straddled more than one parish, also foreigners and those that died at sea.) Mantel's name had been anglicised, just as Handel's had. Armed with the new information, historian Helga Brück in Erfurt, Thuringia, was able to fill in his background. Johann Christian had been the 11th child of a Protestant parson (and brewer) at Gispersleben, a village close to Erfurt. His father lies buried near the altar of the church he served for 45 years.

Both Mantel's early publications refer to him as 'Organist of South Benfleet in the County of Essex'. Later he moved to Great

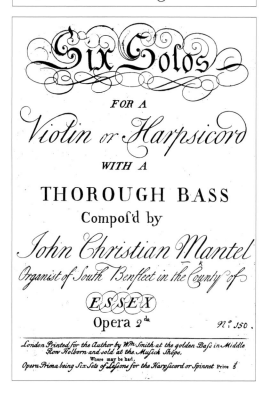

SIX SETTS
of
LESSONS
For the
HARPSICORD or ORGAN
Compos'd by
M: John Christian Mantel
Organist of South-Benfleet in the
County of Essex
Opera Prima
London Printed by W: Smith Musick Printer at
the golden Bass in Middle Row Holborn.

SIX
CONCERT O's
for the
ORGAN or HARPSICHORD,
With Instrumental Parts
Compos'd by
John Christian Mantel
Organist at Great Yarmouth in Nor_
folk, & South Benfleet in Essex:
OP: III.ᵗᵃ N: 14 J: C Mantel.

London *Printed for the Author and sold by* Peter Thompson *at the*
Violin. Hautboy & German Flute the west end of S: Pauls Church-yard.

Where may be had Compos'd by the same Author
Six Sets of Lessons for the Organ or Harpsi-   A Compleat Book of Pfalmody Containing a
chord, Opera Prima ; Price _____ 8:0   variety of Pfalm Tunes, Hymns & Anthems in
Six Solos for a Violin or Harpfichord with a   two three, & four Parts with Additions and
Thorough Bafs, Opera Seconda _____ 5:0   Alterations by Mr James Avifon Price ___ 3:6
Eight Solos for a Violin with a Thorough Bafs   Alfo
& the Harpsichord compos'd by Mr Jos. Gibbs   Publifh'd, the yearly Twenty four Country Dances
__ Dedham in Effex. Price _____ 10:6   for the Violin, German Flute & Hautboy __ 0:6

44   *The Benfleet organist's first publication, 'Six Setts of Lessons ...'*

45   *Second publication, 'Six Solos ...'*

46   *Third publication, 'Six Concertos ...'*

Six Solos
FOR A
Violin or Harpsicord
WITH A
THOROUGH BASS
Compos'd by
John Christian Mantel
Organist of South Benfleet in the County of
ESSEX
Opera 2ᵈᵃ   N: 150.
London Printed for the Author by W: Smith at the golden Bass in Middle
Row Holborn and sold at the Musick Shops.
Where may be had,
Opera Prima being Six Sets of Lessons for the Harpsicord or Spinnet Price 8°

Yarmouth. On the title page of his Opus III, *Six Concertos for the Organ or Harpsichord*, he is described as 'Organist at Great Yarmouth in Norfolk and South Benfleet in Essex'. A stand-in would have taken his place in South Benfleet. Apart from those *Organ Concertos, Six Violin Sonatas* and *Six Suites for Harpsichord* are kept in the British Library. Five unpublished chamber cantatas survive in the Fitzwilliam Museum in Cambridge. In his will he also mentions organ voluntaries and six trio sonatas for two German flutes.

Mantel's music is typical of its time, in the mainstream of the Baroque of Handel and Telemann. The first publication of Mantel's music, *Six Sets of Lessons for Harpsichord or Organ*, contains a list of subscribers which features such personalities as 'Mr Handel' and 'Dr Pepusch', the composer of the *Beggar's Opera*. Francis Clerke's cousin, Miss Bate, then of North Benfleet, is among the list of subscribers to the *Six Organ Concertos*, but not his sister Sarah nor her husband who had inherited the Benfleet estate. (It would seem that Clerke's sister and her husband minimised the obligations of their inheritance. The Clerke memorial inscription on the chancel wall is of lesser quality than that of his wife's, the organ they were looking for was second-hand and it transpires that some of the marble in the chancel floor was slate.)

Could the 'Mr James' on Mantel's list of subscribers be Samuel James of South Benfleet, aged about 22 in 1734, with an estate appraised at £10, which included ownership of Suttons farm? (Samuel James was named executor by Tho. Barber, apothecary/surgeon of South Benfleet in a will approved 21 June 1762.)

A more likely subscriber must be the James James of East Smithfield who became organist in South Benfleet following Mantel's death: '... We, the President and Treasurers of the Corporation of the Governors of the Charity for the relief of the poor widows and children of clergymen, do nominate and appoint James James of East Smithfield in the Parish of St Botolph Aldgate, London, Music Master Organist of the said church of South Benfleet during the pleasure of us or our successors, ... this nineteenth day of October 1764.'

Some intriguing lines in the South Benfleet Parish Accounts Book for 1743, recording an extraordinary meeting in connection with one 'Elexander' Matthews and the 'Prevent Officer', are written in an excellent, small, copperplate handwriting, quite out of character with anything else. It seems to match Mantel's signature on the title sheet for Opus III, the *Organ Concertos*, with good spelling and meticulous execution. This might point to

someone with unusual talents – someone who made a conscious effort to be legible and correct and thereby copied printed type. Equally, the signature on his music is in copperplate handwriting. In the Parish Accounts of 1743 however, signatures of a dozen parishioners and village representatives follow the text, but not, understandably, Mantel's signature, as he was not elected by the parish.

This happened during a period of perceived lack of direction in the village. No vicar or curate signed. The Rev. John Pagett had served until the previous year. His successor, Anthony Cox, does not seem to have attended Vestry meetings. It would appear that the congregation turned for the obligatory entry to their learned organist, who obliged meticulously, but only on that exceptional occasion.

In 1748 John Christian Mantel moved up to Great Yarmouth to play in St Nicholas church one of the best organs in England, 'reputed to have a tone and power second only to the organ at Haarlem in the Netherlands'. His annual salary increased to £40 and yearly benefit concerts added to his standing. Part of his brief was the uplift of Great Yarmouth society and its cultural life as a teacher of music and singing.

Mantel died at the age of 55 on 28 December 1761 and was interred in St Nicholas church in Great Yarmouth. We find a strange parallel with the man whose last will brought him to England – both were the youngest sons of clergymen with extra large families, Clerke the youngest of 14 brothers and one sister, Mantel the younger by six years of 12 siblings.

A Legacy Of Music

Musician David Galbraith, of Leigh-on-Sea, first found reference to Mantel in the British Library in London, intrigued by the local connection. He kindly shared some of his knowledge and findings and in no small measure his infectious enthusiasm. Galbraith has since given concerts of Mantel's music both in South Benfleet and in Mantel's home town of Erfurt.

47   *J.C. Mantel's signature.*

Lately more of Mantel's music has come to light. In 2002 David Galbraith found a manuscript copy of one trio sonata in Lund University Library, Sweden and an organ prelude in Berlin. Violin and cello parts of Mantel's concertos have even turned up in Australia. Mantel's *Six Setts of Lessons for the Harpsichord or Organ* have recently been reprinted by JPH Publications.

On Easter Monday, 27 March 1749, the year following the organist J.C. Mantel's departure, a muddled entry in the Parish Accounts Ledger at the Vestry meeting was resolved by John O'Hara with the autocratic words: 'I appoint John Brewett, senior, church warden ...', the only time such interference by a curate appears. 'John Brewet and James Ford' were the appointed overseers.

End of the Abbey Manor

Following Sarah and Joseph Mayer (also Mayor), the Benfleet lease was held by Samuel Taber in 1759, and by a Jayne Mayor in 1771, followed by the Rev. John Mayor in 1780. According to Benton, in 1799 the Dean and Chapter of St Peter in Westminster sold 'the manor of the Abbey alias South Bemfleet manor, Monkeswyke, Shoreswyke, Hopkeswyke, Sanderswyke, the Rectorial Tithes, and part of a farm called Kent's Hill', to the Rev. John Mayor, 'Rector of Shawbury in the County of Salop'. The Rev. Mayor resold in 1813 to John Perry of Moor Hall, reputedly at a considerable increase in the purchase price from the Dean and Chapter. The two Benfleet manors were now held in the same hands again and in 1833 by John Perry's son, John Watlington Perry. (The Rev. John Mayor was a son of Thomas Mayor of Dolgelly, Merioneth and died in 1826.)

Benfleet's vicar from 1718 to 1742 was John Pagett. He was followed by Anthony Cox (1742-8). Cox was replaced by Thomas Welch (1748-73). Officiating as curates during that period were N. Maund (mentioned 1718), Samuel Asplin (1720), John Beadel in 1735, Samuel Sampson (from 1736), Anthony Neill in 1748 and Joseph O'Hara from 1749. Thos. Biddel, LL.B. was vicar in 1773-4.

Roads and Enclosures

Roads in the Middle Ages often used to be wide, with broad green verges usually to both sides, on which cattle, sheep and horses could be driven, as well as on the narrow gravelled centre strip. This was particularly important on Benfleet clay. Verges were common land like village greens, where locals could pasture their lambs, goats and cows. Pressure on land triggered encroachment on those spaces. In the late 18th century the verges became the targets of squatters who would illegally fence off a small plot. The manorial lord himself might have a hand in such enclosures of what was called the 'Waste'.

The Jarvis Hall court rolls mention as early as 1707 'A parcel of Land where a Cottage once stood abutting on the High Road and on the Graveyard of South Benfleet Church'.

In 1738 we find: '... Brewitt for his shop built on the Waste'.

In 1799 the South Benfleet manor court rolls note: '... the enclosure sometime made by Swan Tabrum esq. upon Hopes Green ... continues. The Bailiff of the said Manor to give notice to Swan Tabrum to remove his corn set thereon, he having received orders to take down the fence set up by Mr Tabrum and lay the same place open to the waste ... within one month from this day.' Swan Tabrum did not take down the fence, nor remove his corn rick.

Again in 1807: 'Also at this Court the Homage present that Robert Loten late of South Benfleet Bargeman, some years since encroached upon the Waste of the said Manor by enclosing part of Hopes Green abutting upon parts of the copyhold Lands this Day surrendered by Withers Jennings to William Snell.'

Swan Tabrum was the lord of the manor of Jarvis Hall from 1787. The Dean and Chapter of St Peter in Westminster had sold 'the manor of the Abbey alias South Bemfleet manor' to the wealthy Rev. John Mayor in 1799-80.

48a *Hopes Green in 1841. It becomes obvious from the layout of the road that much of Hopes Green used to be roadside 'waste', hence the name 'Green', which was then enclosed and cottages were built on the verges. Jarvis land reached south across London Road (now High Road) and Hall Farm land extended to the north of it.*

48b *Tarpots Corner in 1841. Squatters had moved onto the verge of what is now the A13 London Road before it reaches Bread and Cheese Hill to the east. (Both illustrations based on the Benfleet Tithe Map)*

Here we witness the interesting development of a tussle between the Benfleet manor and the 'pretended manor' of Jarvis Hall whose court under Swan Tabrum sat more regularly and was quite liberal in granting plots of land from the 'waste' along roads and later at Dawes Heath.

One of the more elusive characters from that time is carpenter Simon Daines. He managed to avoid being named in the parish accounts and never took up a vestry office, but by collecting grants of land along the roads and erecting 'messuages' on them, while ignoring South Benfleet court orders to vacate them, he built up a small empire of 13 cottages, besides the Hopes Green land, a Butcher's House in East

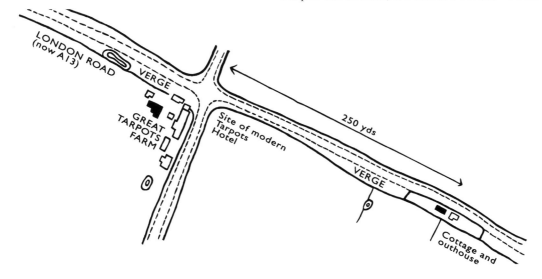

49 *'Mayes on the Waste' cottages at the upper end of East Street, now Essex Way. One at least was known as Mrs Carter's Cottage, early in the 20th century. Both cottages were demolished.*
   a) *Looking east.*
   b) *Looking west.*

Street and two cottages he had built on a piece of land next the churchyard.

Most of Hopes Green disappeared between 1792 and 1804, and has since been lost completely. Thus many of the shops that line the High Road in South Benfleet stand on former roadside verges.

Some cottages had to come down again. The South Benfleet tithe map of 1841 shows a cottage and outhouse on the verge in what is now the London Road, some 250 yards east of Tarpots junction, and in Essex Way, almost opposite the bottom of Norwood Drive, were two cottages known as Mayes on the 'Waste'. The first was mentioned in 1739. In 1869 John Pritchard, brewer of Southend, acquired them for £35 and bought the property out of copyhold.

We have seen how often people had to be taken to court for not repairing their sections of roads or for not scouring out the ditches beside them. It was the thankless task of the surveyor of highways to view the parish roads, bridges and watercourses three times a year and report to the Justices. The heavy clay of Benfleet was a real problem, 'stiff, numb, dumb and impervious', particularly on damp days. Faggots were cut and bundled and laid down before being covered with stones and gravel as soakaways to help dry out the surface.

Benfleet needed lots of stones. Apart from the hoy-loads brought over from Kent, high ground like Hadleigh Common and Lady Dunlop's fields around Jarvis Hall gave employment to a number of people, paupers, old people and children gathering stones, piling and screening. Shovels, picks and sieves were provided by the parish. In 1799 Lady Dunlop supplied '100 loads of stone at 2s. 6d. a load and 18 loads of the best at 5s. a load'. When a road became too rutted and uneven, a harrow might have to be dragged over it: '20 October 1798. Harrowing the Road 5s. For dragging the Road with 4 Horses and 2 Men 15s.'

Up on high gravel ground like Thundersley roads were less of a problem, though down at Tarpots roads ran on clay and Thundersley parish was fined £50 in 1784 and again in 1805. In 1802 they acted quickly to forestall a fine of £100.

Turnpikes were set up by acts of Parliament on trunk roads where upkeep had become unfair to small parishes. The tollhouse at Victoria House Corner on the road through Benfleet via Tarpots and Bread and Cheese Hill lasted into recent times.

As late as the end of the 18th century a wooden bridge near the church needed to be kept in good repair and at Hopes Green, besides a ford for wagon and horses, there was a brick-based footbridge to maintain: '40 bushels of lime for the arches on the Wharf and Hopes Green £1 6s. 8d. Mr Turner for carting £2 10s. Bricklayers Bill £8 17s. 1d. To Barrows and Planks 3s.'

Bread and Cheese Hill

The *Bread and Cheese Inn* supplies sustenance on Bread and Cheese Hill, a local name for which there are several explanations. The Rev. A.B. Maley returned to Henry de Essex, standard-bearer to King Henry II and Lord of the Honour of Rayleigh, for his interpretation. On a campaign for the king in Wales the army was ambushed at Consyth in Flintshire, where the Welsh fell on them with the battle cry 'Baru Caws'. Back in Thundersley, it is said, Henry's retainers found such a resemblance between the place their Welsh assailants had chosen and the defile on the south side of Coombe Wood, they called it Baru Caws Hill.

The Rev. W.E. Heygate, in the Essex Revue of 1892, placed the origins of the name to the Peasants' Revolt of 1381. Flemings were particularly hated at the time and when the rebels suspected a man of being a Fleming, they tested him with the words 'Bread and Cheese'. If he pronounced the trial words as 'Brode and Case' (brood en kaas) he was presumed to be a foreigner and killed. They got to be known as Bread and Cheese Men and later, when they were pursued by the king's men, they occupied the high and wooded ground and quite likely the steep ground close to Jarvis Hall …

Another possible explanation is the connection of sheep with the lords of Jarvis Hall. The shepherds' sustenance would consist largely of bread and cheese made from the milk of the thousands of sheep. Thus the house of their employers stood on Bread and Cheese Hill. But maybe it was quite simply the many hawthorn trees that lined the steep road on both sides, that supplied the name. In folklore the hawthorn is also known as the bread and cheese tree …

Walking the Bounds

Walking the Bounds of the South Benfleet parish was recorded in 1834, when the Vestry met at 9 o'clock in the morning of 21 May on Cliff Hill, walked across the uplands to lunch at Jarvis Hall, thence to Poynetts Dock and back to dine at the *Hoy*. The same went on the next day, when 20 posts were 'put down at their proper points'. That evening they dined at the *Anchor*.

VII

Victorian Benfleet

Vicars and Organs

The Rev. John Phelps (1837-45) was responsible for starting the village school and the church was reseated during his incumbency.

The (new) vicarage on the High Road, at the bottom of Vicarage Hill, was 'pulled down' by the Rev. Henry Lloyd (1845-50) and a new one erected a little further up the hill – now a private house known as the Old Vicarage. Above that, today's vicarage is therefore at least the fourth building of that description in South Benfleet. Lloyd also planted the avenue of sycamore trees in the churchyard.

An entry in the parish magazine in October 1897 referred to undated alterations to the interior of St Mary's: '… the organ was removed from the gallery apparently in the west end to its present position. The galleries were taken away, the floors lowered to the original level, all this and much more was done, through the efforts of Mr Henderson [the Rev. Thomas Julius Henderson, M.A., 1859-73], who was, it is said, a born architect.' The rood stair in the thickness of the north wall was built about 1380. It gave difficult access to the old rood loft and gallery. Structural damage from the supports of that earlier gallery is still visible in the north aisle.

South Benfleet church accounts contain a reference to a more recent new organ than that

50   *The Vicarage, now the 'Old Vicarage', on Vicarage Hill, c.1915.*

51 *Late 14th-century steps in St Mary's north wall. The filled-in doorway, left, has been re-opened in 2005.*

52 *Church interior, c.1912. On the south wall is the Clerke monumental plaque. The organ has since been placed against the tower at the back of the church.*

bequeathed by Francis Clerke. It was ordered by the vicar, the Rev. C.F. Box (1895-1914). The builders were H. Jones & Sons of South Kensington and the cost was £189. Of that amount £155 had been 'paid from a sum saved by the Rev. W.E. Spence (1885-1895) from the Organ Benefaction yielding £30 yearly, £13 the value of the old organ and subscriptions brought in by the Vicar'.

In the tower of the church were kept copies of the parish magazine since the end of the 19th century. They are now in the Essex Record Office. The fragile pages of the first bound volume contain mentions of the old organ. In November 1897 the acquisition of a new one was announced, confirming the church accounts.

None of the firms of organ builders was interested in acquiring the old organ. Over the years it had been 'shamefully treated and tampered with by inefficient repairers ... Some of the pipes ... have been treated in the same way as the human ear to prevent taking cold

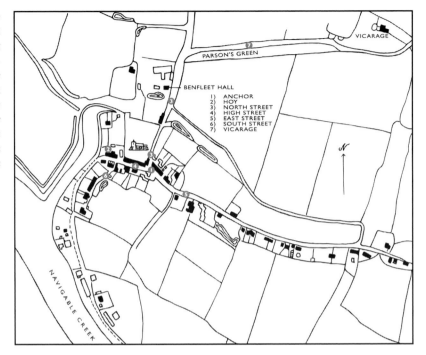

53 The Benfleet Tithe Map of 1841 gives a good idea of the extent of the village for hundreds of years. At the end of Church Creek was a space where hoys could turn. (Map size 9ft 9½in deep, 6ft 5in wide. The copy held in Council offices is even larger.)

– stopped up with tow, and moreover, rags have been used to keep the wind within the bellows.'

Benton reports that the organ in his time (1867) had been built by Gower of Kingsland Road, London, which might well be that very instrument.

The purchaser the vicar found 'anticipates making a new organ of it, or at least rebuilding it at a profit ...' A local story tells of the old organ disappearing up Bread and Cheese Hill eastwards on a horse and cart.

The new organ was opened on Saturday, 27 November 1898, at four o'clock on a 'boisterous' afternoon 'with a goodly number of parishioners and visitors present ...' That organ stood fine and upright against the north wall of the chancel until it was rebuilt and moved to today's position high against the tower wall at the rear of the church, in the 1920s.

Benfleet Before the Railway

In 1841 most of South Benfleet was still concentrated around the church, up East Street and down High Street to the 'Hard'. In addition

54 South Street, now 'The Close', post-First World War.

to the inns, two wheelwrights, two grocers, two butchers and a cordwainer (cobbler) shared the High Street.

An easily missed narrow lane, no more than a footpath opposite the church, now called 'The Close', used to be South Street, or just The Alley, where a farmer's agent, three more shoemakers, a poulterer, a blacksmith, a dressmaker and a carrier were situated, with the smithy across the road next to the *Hoy*. Another shoemaker and a 'salesman' were sited in East Street, a tailor and a baker by the bridge at the north end of the churchyard, and just one carpenter at Hopes Green.

A cryer would have broadcast anything of instant concern to the population. In 1837, during a rabies scare, we find a note explaining how such news was broadcast to the village: '…This notice to be cryed in the usual manner.' In 1841 nine hoymen were listed in the village and *White's Directory* of 1848 mentioned that the creek in the vicinity was celebrated for oysters.

The Eastern Counties Railway Extension in its Book of Reference defined everything that lay in its proposed path in 1846. The map gives precise information of what there was on the ground, who owned it and who lived there. Every salting, marsh, field, cottage and outbuilding, garden shed and drying ground

is listed, though only on the southern rim of the parish.

Perhaps surprisingly, that part of Benfleet belonged to just a few families at the time. Starting at the parish boundary with Pitsea, several fields, paddock and outbuildings belonged to William Hilton, junior. (William Hilton of Danbury and later his son George were also major landholders on Canvey Island.)

Moving east, the next owner of fields, marsh and saltings was Jeremiah Rosher, who also shared the creek with Henry and Jonathan Wood, both senior. Henry Wood, senior, owned saltings, at least fifteen cottages or houses with gardens and outbuildings, a shop, granary, wharf, field and orchard. Jonathan Wood, senior, owned a house, a cottage and a garden, workshop, wharf and outbuildings, yard and coal yard.

Daniel Nash was the owner of two kilns, two wharfs, a coal shed, granary, cottages (two unfinished), timber yard, workshop, fields and saltings. John Henry Nash owned a field, marshes and saltings as well as the Ferry House, which was ascribed to James Salesbury, who must have been the ferryman. Salesbury lived in one of Henry Wood's cottages in the village. (An Adam Nash had been recorded in Benfleet as one of 12 jurors in 1412, surely a family of some considerable duration, though the land-

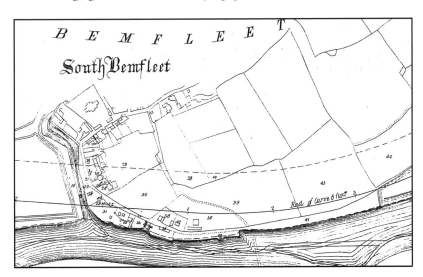

55 *Eastern Counties Railway, Book of Reference, 1846, shows the southern half of Benfleet with the properties affected by the planned railway line. It also shows the traditional route to Canvey, along School Lane, and a field owned by Daniel Nash. At that time even the railway still spelled the name 'Bemfleet'.*

owning Nashes seem to have different abodes every time they're mentioned.)

The 'Master, Fellows and Scholars of Kings College, Cambridge' were owners of marshland to the east along the edge of the land, followed by marsh of the Trustees of Enfield Charity to and across the parish boundary with Hadleigh.

The map shows the buildings that stood in the way of the new railway line. Some of the cottages and outbuildings to the south of the railway survived until the Canvey underpass was built, but the houses lining the creek near the *Hoy*, so fondly remembered in early 20th-century photographs, had yet to be erected.

A Saintly Vicar and the Railway Age

The London, Tilbury and Southend Railway line from Forest Gate to Barking, Rainham, Purfleet, Grays, Tilbury Fort (for the docks and the pleasure gardens at Rosherville near Gravesend), Pitsea, Benfleet, and Leigh-on-Sea was opened in 1856. It had reached Southend that same year. At Benfleet a large embankment was necessary to straddle the marshy land from Pitsea and to squeeze around the high ground of the Downs. Originally, only a single line was planned for this section, though changes were authorised in June 1854: 'stations between Thames Haven Junction and Leigh should be constructed as for a double line...'. The Stanford-le-Hope to Leigh section was opened on Sunday 1 July 1855, including the stations at Pitsea and Benfleet. The second line was brought into use in May 1856, so that the whole of the line was double track. The Barking to Pitsea extension was completed more than 30 years later, and the final East Horndon to Pitsea section opened on 1 June 1888.

When the Sickness Struck

The year was 1854 when the railway line was under construction past South Benfleet, raising the rails across the marshes, bridging Church Creek and the 'Hard' and on alongside Hadleigh Ray. Benfleet's original wooden station was sited a little further east from today's station, nearer

the crossing to Canvey. Pubs and cottages in the small village were crowded with lodgers.

Skeletons and charred timbers of Viking ships were found during the excavations – remnants from the battle King Alfred's men fought and won here in A.D. 893 – preserved in the deep Thames mud. Given the events at the time, it is perhaps not surprising that none of those items survived, for it was also the year that cholera visited England for the last time. Ten thousand still died of the epidemic in London before its source was identified. It did not spare South Benfleet.

'The pestilence fell like a thunderbolt upon the parish of Benfleet...' is how the Rev. W.E. Heygate described the arrival of the sickness in his harrowing account of the life of Benfleet's vicar at that time.

One old woman who had been nursing the sick died at her task. Her husband and the niece who lived with them quickly followed. The man who took on the burden of nursing was the vicar, the Rev. John Aubone Cook, 'visiting the sick and dying from week's end to week's end. For seven whole days and nights he never went to his bed. For nearly three weeks he had not one whole night's rest.'

Cook was doctor and counsellor in one, neglecting to eat as he rushed from house to house, sometimes spending as much as 16 hours without food, 'administering the medicines, rubbing the cold limbs of those in collapse and praying by them when they were conscious ...'

A physician of body and soul, not only did he tend to his own parishioners, but also the labourers who swelled their ranks. 'There was no office so loathsome, but he himself executed it,' Heygate wrote later. 'With his own hands he held, carried, removed, cleansed, brought again the vessels required in such disease. The effluvia in a room occupied by several of these coarse men, labouring under such a nauseous sickness as cholera, must have been overpowering. He lived in it ...'

Cook himself buried those he had nursed.

In Benfleet's Register of Burials of that time, the horror stares out from the pages. In a period from 23 September to 16 October 1854 alone, there were 38 fatalities. Only six days in that period record no burials – some days indicate three, one even four. Ages range from two months to 79 years, but strikingly obvious are the number of young men in their twenties and thirties.

The vicar's sad recordings of each day's undertakings show a remarkable consistency. He simply did what had to be done to the best of his ability.

John Aubone Cook

John Aubone Cook was born 29 December 1811 at Pilgrim's Hatch near Brentwood in Essex, the son of a colonel of a cavalry regiment, the 28th Light Dragoons. Very early in his life the family moved to France, to a village nine miles from Le Havre by the side of the Seine. There, as he grew up, he would join his father on shooting expeditions, which in some ways prepared him for his later, peripatetic ministry.

He spoke perfect French. His first school was at Havre de Grace, followed by the French College at Honfleur, before his education continued in Woolwich in England.

When his father died in 1829, his brother joined the Army. John Aubone went to seek his fortune in India, but soon returned. On the return journey a storm almost wrecked and dismasted the ship. Perhaps it was then that his future was decided. Cook entered Corpus Christi College in Cambridge in 1834. He had much to catch up on, but by Christmas 1838 he was ordained by the Bishop of London. Not much is recorded about the man himself, but an illness in 1840 left him with a weakness in his voice which made delivery irregular, at times indistinct.

The new vicarage 'some distance from the village up a hill' – known today as the Old Vicarage – was unfinished when Cook arrived. One parishioner was recorded as saying: 'If ever there was a man who cared for the souls of his people, it was he…' When times returned to normal, following the cholera visitation, grateful survivors presented Cook not with something personal, but with 'a beautiful set of vessels for administering the Holy Communion to the sick'.

Cook replaced Henry Robert Lloyd as vicar in 1850, coming from 12 years' ministry as curate of St Margaret's near the Houses of Parliament. There, in London in 1849, he had lived through one such epidemic already, visiting the sick and burying 50 people in one week. Fourteen thousand died during that outbreak.

In 1852 he was made Rural Dean of Canewdon, another job without remuneration, involving expense and long walks. In December 1857 he also took on Canvey and for six months he served Benfleet and the island alone.

His biographer was adamant: 'This poor benefice, which in good years yielded only £200 clear of outgoings, was all he ever received in the church until he accepted the incumbency of Canvey Island, for its sake, not his own, thus adding to his labours and not his income, for he paid his assistant curate all that he received, and brought himself to his grave.'

Heygate describes Canvey Island as a 'deposit of the Thames, existing in some form as early as the second century of the Christian era … It was enlarged over the years … The population is small, but scattered. There is a chapel upon it …'.

Cook continued to assist widows and beggars to the detriment of his own health. Unlike some clergy, he encouraged people to send for him at all hours of the day or night. He ate little. Even when gifts such as game arrived, he was prone to give them away. As his own health faltered, he suffered frequent attacks of neuralgia.

Death of a Good Man

On 7 May 1859 he presided over the Vestry meeting for the last time. A hot summer was followed by an unusual degree of sickness. In a letter to a friend, Cook wrote: 'The sickness is fearful, general, almost universal. I am obliged to be both doctor and parson. I have never been so hard-worked since the cholera was here. People are seized with diarrhoea, pains in the limbs, sickness and fever, with a black tongue.'

On Saturday, 10 September, he undertook his last day of parochial visiting. He left home at mid-day and went from house to house without food. Darkness fell as he was still on the island. He lost his way and did not arrive home until ten that night. He felt ill, but Sunday lay ahead, which meant a full service at Benfleet in the morning, at Canvey in the afternoon and Benfleet again in the evening. With feverish pain in his head, he forced himself through the day's work, then took to his bed. He was very ill for several days.

Many recovered from such fever and the attending medical man expected him to improve. Maybe he was too weak. The fever seems to have affected his brain, leaving him delirious. He died on 'the Feast of St Michael and All Angels', the very day on which, five years earlier, he had buried four victims of the cholera. His aged mother and eldest sister were with him at the end.

56 *Tombstones of J.A. Cook, his mother and sister, by the south porch.*

On Sunday, 2 October 1859, the Rev. Heygate from Southend spoke at Cook's graveside as parishioners lowered his oak coffin. Heygate wrote later: 'There were no dry eyes. I never saw so many weep, nor so worthily.' John Aubone Cook rests from his labours close to St Mary's beautiful south porch, flanked on either side by his mother and his sister. He had helped preserve the porch when the Vestry were considering taking it down, as even then it was in danger of falling to ruin.

Inside the church, at the side of the altar, a brass wall plaque reminds us of his sacrifice. But the large east window above the altar, which had been dedicated to his memory and featured the Good Samaritan, has since had to be replaced. It fell victim to a more recent, man-made calamity: 'The glass in this window was inserted in 1948 to replace that presented by parishioners in memory of the Rev. John Aubone Cook, Vicar of South Benfleet from 1850 to 1859, which was destroyed by enemy action on the night of 12 October, 1940.'

Cook's biographer described Benfleet in enthusiastic Victorian terms, but there is a sting in the tail: 'It lies beautifully varied with hill and dale and commands the sweetest views of the Thames, Kent, Essex, and on the east, of the sea. On the south however lies Canvey Island, and on the west a tract of marsh, very picturesque with light and shade, especially at sunset and in harvest, but equally unhealthy…'

Thomas Julius Henderson, M.A.

Thomas Julius Henderson (1859-73), of Wadham College, Oxford, formerly curate at Messing, Hadleigh and Leigh, replaced John Aubone Cook. He brought with him his wife, daughter of Captain Brand the Leigh Revenue Officer, and a small daughter.

Under Vicar Henderson the hammerbeam church porch was repaired, the floor of the nave was lowered back to the level of pre-Puritan times, the west gallery was taken down, a new organ was placed in the chancel and the vestry was opened in the tower. Like his predecessor,

57 *St Mary's east window as it is today, a replacement for the original Cook window.*

he seems to have been very active on behalf of the church and his parishioners, but after eight years he fell victim to the ague, now known as malaria, and was advised to leave the parish on health grounds.

Census Records

Estimated population figures for South Benfleet show that numbers remained fairly static until after 1750, when populations grew generally. The first census was made in 1801. In the next 40 years population figures more than doubled from 338 in 1801 to 707 in 1841. Why figures fluctuated is unclear, but the following decade

saw the number of inhabitants down again to 570. The decade that includes the cholera outbreak ended with an increase of three in the population. Recovery was very slow: 573 for 1861, 586 for 1871, 681 for 1881. Numbers went down slightly to 569 for 1891.

Benfleet's dramatic growth began at the turn of the century – in 1901 the census reports 1,024; ten years later the figure was 1,305. In the years between the wars the population rose from 1,918 in 1921 to 4,170 in 1931.

The Napoleonic Wars had made the growing of corn profitable and the Downs and Canvey would have been under the plough. Wheat was 'the golden crop' in terms of profitability. Nationally, from 1815 corn prices had to be protected by the Corn Laws. When these laws were repealed in 1844, prices were depressed, labourers lost their jobs and had to seek work elsewhere.

Resident at the *Hoy* in 1841, apart from the innkeeper's family of four and two servants, were eight agricultural labourers. By 1851 a different landlord with wife, father and one servant were complemented by four lodgers.

Benfleet did not rely solely on agriculture, though most of the churchwardens in the mid-1800s were still farmers: Daniel Nash owned Suttons; James Potter of Reeds Hill, George Osborn Andrews of Jarvis Hall, Michael Wood of Great Tarpots, William Sopwith of Sweet Briar Farm and, as an exception, Henry Lucking, landlord of the *Anchor*, were among the overseers of the poor.

Miss Henderson, Vicar Henderson's daughter, still remembered Canvey and the Downs 'golden with corn and fields of mustard' in the 1860s–70s.

The Railways

The railways replaced the convenience of the harbour in the movement of people and goods, and also replaced some of the jobs lost on the barges. The sad events in Benfleet of 1854, when the railway line via Tilbury was built, have been described above (see p.58).

Dickens' *Dictionary of the Thames (from Oxford to the Nore)* of 1880 gave the time from London to Benfleet on the London, Tilbury and Southend Railway as about one hour 30 minutes. Fares to London (single and return) were: 1st Class, 3s. 9d., 6s. 3d.; 2nd Class, 2s. 10d., 4s. 9d.; 3rd Class, 1s. 11d., 3s. 10d. In 1888 the connection from Barking to Pitsea was completed, crossing Bulphan Fen, thus shortening the journey to London to about three quarters of an hour.

Census records of the second half of the 19th century show a changing Benfleet. As a result of the railway, Station Road became prominent. In 1861 Graham Wise was Stationmaster, living in Station Road with his family and a railway porter and wife as subtenants. Ten years later, Frank H.J. Tomkins with wife and two children held that office.

Robert Townshend, at 48, was stationmaster by 1881 and lived there with his wife Sarah, five children and a lodger, John Fox, a schoolmaster. Mobility in following jobs had increased considerably by then. The Townshends originally came from Norwich, where their eldest son was born; a daughter was born in Suffolk and the next three children in Braintree. The lodger was born in Leicestershire. Ten years later the stationmaster's name had changed again.

Also listed in Station Road in 1881 – in the shop opposite the railway station – was postmistress Elizabeth Brewitt, widowed at 49, with three sons and a daughter, a domestic servant and five boarders, one of whom was a railway guard. Her late husband Henry had been listed as boot maker and church clerk ten years earlier.

Besides the railway guard, a porter, a signalman and a railway plate layer were resident in Benfleet – no railway workers had been listed at the previous count.

Changes in the Village

There were no houses by the creek near the *Hoy* in 1846. The weatherboarded houses we see in early photographs were probably erected – on

58   *Harry Robert Townshend, Benfleet station-master, c.1880. (Picture supplied by his great-great-granddaughters Paddy and Bobby.)*

barges or stilts – when buildings had to make way for the arrival of the railway. They were not built to withstand high spring tides, which were prone to surge into the backs of these homes, out through their fronts and across the road into the houses on the opposite side of lower High Street.

It was a busy area. At addresses given as 'The Wharf' at the time of the 1861 census there were seven households which included a barge master, bargeman, sailmaker, ship's carpenter, bargeman's wife, wharfinger's wife and a governess. 'Wharf House', later known as Mrs Wheeler's cottage, was in 1861 the home of Mary Anne Howard, a barge-owner's widow. Her eldest son William was barge owner, his brother Israel was barge master and their 24-year-old sister Margaret was described as 'barge master's daughter'. With daughters-in-law, a grandchild, and two young 'visitors', there were

59 *View from the railway station, 1913. Houses and business premises on stilts had been established along the 'Hard'.*

60 *By the side and at the back of the* Hoy *still stand the buildings of the sawmill, c.1925. In front of the* Hoy *at this angle is Mrs Wheeler's cottage, 'Wharf House'. On the right, the black weatherboarded semi-detached home of Nurse Revell next door to the Killingbacks. Dominating the high ground to the left of the church tower is Boyce Hill farmhouse.*

nine people living at 'Wharf House'. In the village altogether a dozen families plus various lodgers still had connections to the wharf.

Simon Daines, a 68-year-old carpenter, held the Post Office. In 1871 he is again recorded as Postmaster, a widower living on High Street. At the same time a Charles Daines, at 44, was 'beer seller' at the *Crown* and a 65-year-old Thomas Daines lived in Endway, suffering from epilepsy, probably in one of the poorhouses. Several widows are listed as receiving parish relief. Peter Bell of the High Street, while not cited as receiving parish alms, was recorded as being paralysed at 64 years of age. His wife, 27 years his junior, would have had to support their four daughters, all under seven, the youngest just four months.

Farms were still strongly represented, most with large families and labourers living in. James Cheeseman of Suttons Farm counted barge owner among his activities. At Reeds Hill widow Caroline Potter farmed 185 acres with six men and three boys, and William E. Benton worked Hobly Thick Farm's 287 acres with the same complement of men and boys. Abraham Talbot at Tarpot's (165 acres), made do with four men and three boys.

Ten years later, in 1871, while fewer farms are mentioned, the number of households with connections to the wharf remained static.

With the spiritual well-being of the village of utmost Victorian importance, Thomas J. Henderson occupied the vicarage with his wife Francisca and their 14-year-old daughter Francis. The sturdy house on Vicarage Hill was also home to two old ladies, a pupil, a cook, a housemaid and a groom.

Domestic service was still one of the few occupations for women in the village. The *Hoy* employed the youngest female servant at 12 years of age.

All three of the village inns could accommodate lodgers. By 1881 George Land, his wife Sarah, their three sons and a daughter had taken over the *Anchor*. William Warner was innkeeper at the *Hoy* with wife Mahala,

a niece listed as barmaid, and a nephew who tended the inn's horses as 'hostler'.

The growth industry locally in that decade was the brickfields. Of 55 brick makers mentioned in the census, seven, all from Surrey and Middlesex, were lodging at the *Hoy*.

In the creek six occupants were recorded on four barges and nine crew from Middlesex stayed on four fishing smacks.

Farms remained the biggest employers in 1881: John Harvey worked the 70 acres of Suttons Farm with three men and one woman, while on Reeds Hill farmer Joseph Augustus Browne managed over twice the acreage –180 – with six men and two boys, a domestic servant and a young gardener by the name of Henry Brewett.

Seventy-year-old Abraham Talbot farmed the 220-acre Great Tarpots Farm with the help of four men, two women and three boys. Equally at 70, farm bailiff John Parish ran Boyce Hill Farm with his wife, four sons and a granddaughter and a grandson described as a 'sweep'.

Elsewhere the agricultural depression had begun in the 1870s. Generally, Benfleet seems to have been bucking the trend. The census of the last decade in the 19th century, 5 April 1891, saw 81 people still earning their living on the land. Add to that number two shepherds and four haybinder/thatchers, 11 general labourers, nine bargees and fishermen, and a dozen railway employees.

Remarkably, brick makers were down to 11, though there was a new, potentially more dangerous, way of earning a living. With powder hulks moored offshore from Holehaven Point towards Pitsea, five 'magazine keepers' are listed, including a foreman. (There was even talk of gunpowder being stored in caves in Benfleet Creek.) As nearby Pitsea saw the setting-up of a munitions factory on 200 acres of marshland in 1890, those men may quite possibly have contributed to the defence of British interests in the Boer Wars in South Africa.

Another surprise entry for 1891 was a printer/machine manager. Benfleet may have

61 *Drawing by Sir Charles Nicholson, 'architect and preserver of so many churches old and new' in St Mary's church. Not a literal representation, but perhaps as he would like to have seen it (c.1898).*

been resisting change, but modern times were approaching.

The Artistic Nicholsons

Benfleet has always attracted benefactors. Sir Charles Archibald Nicholson, Bart (1867-1949) and Lady Nicholson lie near the tower, west of the south porch of St Mary's church. As a church architect he took great interest in the church and its history. In 1927 he gave a talk in the church entitled: 'Our wonderful Old Church' and in 1928 he published a four-part historical article in the parish magazine: 'St Mary's by the Pirate's Creek'.

Sir Charles and his brothers, Archibald Keightley, master glass painter, and Dr Sidney Hugo Nicholson, who was organist of Westminster Abbey and founder of the Royal School of Church Music, were responsible for repairs and alterations 'in memory of their parents', comprising the reseating and restoration of the north aisle, the renovation of the organ erected in 1897, and the insertion of fine modern stained glass in the windows of the south aisle. On 19 November 1899 'bells were rung for the first time in nine years after restoration'. The nave roof was raised in 1902.

It was certainly a family effort. Apart from Sir Charles, who was the church's architect from *c.*1890–1949, and his brothers, his wife Lady Nicholson painted the reredos behind the high altar in 1891 and his daughter Miss B. Nicholson painted the saints on the base of the new rood screen in a medieval style.

Sir Charles was born in Hadleigh House, where the parish boundary passed through the porch. The restoration architect, historian and benefactor of St Mary's church is remembered in Nicholson Avenue off Shipwrights Drive, near his former home.

62 *Modern church interior.*

63 *View down Station Road, c.1925. The first house on the right was Miss Howard's School.*

Dame Schools to National

Thirty children were educated in 'dame schools' in Benfleet in 1810. William Sopwith, sometime overseer of the poor, rented of Jonathan Wood all the land between the present Grove Road and Vicarage Hill, as well as owning cottages on roadside waste at Hopes Green and in East Street. He lived with his wife, son, two daughters and a servant in Sweet Briar Farm of 140 acres. *White's Directory* of 1848 cites Miss Caroline Elizabeth Sopwith, probably his daughter, as running a private school 'with two boarders and a servant'. The 1841 census also mentions William Potter as parish clerk and schoolmaster, obviously not particularly well remunerated occupations, for by 1851 he was listed as an 'infirm pauper', aged 76.

64 *A reminder of Benfleet's waterside activities, c.1913. T.E. Ross, builders merchant, later became W.T. Lamb. In 1908 Thos. E. Ross, of the Wharf, advertised as house, estate and apartment agent: 'Plots! Plots! In Excellent Positions suitable for Shops, etc. Several Small Estates for Sale!' On the rise, background right, on what is now the car park, we get a glimpse of the old school.*

65 *Hopes Green School, 1926. The brook divides the school from the tennis courts behind Benfleet Hall, later the Country Club. The building at an angle on the corner of Brook Road and High Road, now gone, was at one time a cinema. Note how the boundaries fit the Tithe Map of 1841. (See page 51, Little Brook Field)*

First National School

On the corner of East Street and School Lane, just below Suttons Farm, a Methodist church had stood since 1877. Higher up on the former Glebe Lane to Canvey, on the west side, the National School's two buildings were established in 1845 on a site given by Mr Wood. Its first mistress, at the beginning of systematic teaching within the parish, lasted only a few months. Her successor stayed just one month (8 April – 8 May 1846), after which the trustees appointed Elizabeth Freeman. The census of 1861 still lists her as schoolmistress, a widow of 62, with her daughter Sarah as assistant. 21-year-old Rose Plowright was schoolmistress in 1871.

Westminster Abbey, as patrons, picked up the bills for equipment. As a Church of England School, its accent was on religious studies. School hours were Monday to Saturday, nine

STANLEY HOUSE SCHOOL
LONDON ROAD   ::   SOUTH BENFLEET

Kindergarten & Preparatory School
::   for Girls and Boys   ::
Pupils prepared for High Schools

Principal—Miss M. E. STEGGLES, A.T.C.L.,
                        Teacher's Training Diploma,
Assisted by—Miss M. JONES, Lond. Matric.

Prospectus on application to Principal.

66   *Advertisement from the Annual Carnival and Fête Programme, 1935.*

to five, with a two-hour midday break. The curriculum included, besides the 'three R's', singing, chanting and of course religious study. In 1894 the diocesan inspector's comments were: 'Imperfect ventilation, unsuitable desks and overcrowding. English is wanting in thoroughness.' Robert Hall was organist and headmaster for 30 years from 1893 to 28 March 1923.

The first important Education Act created a Board of Education in 1870 and put all schools under the supervision of the state. More council schools were built and in 1926 the Benfleet National School was abandoned for the South Benfleet Primary Council School,

a new and better building (in the High Road, almost opposite the bottom of Kents Hill Road), though the old school was used by the parish until 1931.

East Street became Essex Way and the site of the school is today part of the station car park. A new Methodist church was opened in the High Road, at the bottom of Vicarage Hill, on 8 April 1931.

Local Administration

In the 1850s the South Benfleet Vestry still ordered staves and handcuffs for the parish constables and the parish cage was still in use. But times were changing and Vestry responsibilities started to decline. Health and Highway Boards were established, education and public health acts, centralisation of poor relief in unions of parishes and the abolition of compulsory church rates (1868) had their effects, albeit slowly.

The first South Benfleet Parish Council was elected on Tuesday, 4 December 1894 under the provisions of the Local Government Act of that year. The first elected councillors, who met at the Village Institute on the churchyard by the light of paraffin lamps, were Nicholson, Francis, Browne, Revell, Attwell, Howard and Lawrence. Chairman was the vicar, the Rev. W.E. Spencer. Later the meetings were held in the schoolroom.

Canvey became a separate parish in 1881.

67   *Church Corner before the War Memorial was built – the Village Institute is centre left, with Knightleys and the* Anchor *with a high-wheeled cart for transport. Only the* Anchor *and the shops on the extreme left have survived.*

VIII

Early in the
Twentieth Century

The Parish Council lasted for 35 years until 1 October 1929, when Thundersley and Hadleigh joined together to form the Benfleet Urban District Council. Though each parish had its own parish council prior to 1929, they had formed part of the Rural District of Rochford. The Vestry carried on, though all that was left were parochial matters and, for a while, the custody of parish registers and records.

The Canvey Connection

A hundred years ago access to Canvey Island was still either by stepping stones at low tide or at other times by ferry. Tide tables governed the traffic and were published by local papers and in council guidebooks. In emergencies there was always the bell to summon the ferryman, night or day, at the Ferry House nearby. Two punts

and two row-boats denoted the ferry. The fare was one penny (1d.) – tuppence would include your bicycle.

Larger vehicles, wagons and horses, coal wagons and carts, could find crossing more problematic if they had misjudged the time and left it late. Cows and horses have been swept away by the surging tide. Cars might have to be abandoned, to be rescued by horses and the ferryman.

On Bank Holidays the steam trains would bring large crowds on day excursions, especially from the East End of London.

The Plotlands Idea

This grew out of a combination of the depressed price of farm land, the spread of 'holiday' and 'weekend' habits, and an increasing property-

68 *Stepping stones to Benfleet, late 1920s. Controversial poster hoardings, ferryman's hut and floating Yacht Club premises in the background. The Dutch gabled house on the ridge top right, Brecon House, was built early in the 20th century by the Barnes family who owned Suttons Farm. It is built of flint, rather than brick or wood.*

69 *A holiday scene near the ferryman's hut while waiting to cross over to Canvey, c.1925-6. The Canvey Supply Co. Ltd advertised timber and builders' merchandise.*

70 *A precarious journey. The fare was one penny – tuppence if you took your bike.*

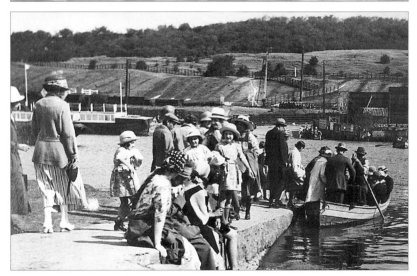

71 *Returning was equally problematic, but for some just part of the fun.*

72 *At low tide the journey might be improved by a 'boneshaker' bus, mid-1920s.*

73 *A busy day at the Ferry, c.1925. Three boats are trying to cope with the queue on the Canvey side.*

owning democracy. It turned Canvey into a place of escape for smog-ridden Londoners. Sales techniques such as promises of a free meal, a free rail ticket to genuine purchasers of plots of land ('… prominent positions from 30/- per plot'), and maybe a Christmas turkey added to the deal, brought in the crowds, who then defiantly ignored existing building codes.

Canvey had it's own entrepreneur, Frederick B. Hester, who attempted to turn the island into a seaside residential holiday resort with a European flavour – 'Little Holland'. 1,004 plots of land were laid out on part of Leigh Beck Farm in 1901 and for several years an intensive holiday development took place on the island. Whitsun 1904 saw a successful land auction and 2,000 visitors arrived in July that year. The elaborate plans led to Hester's bankruptcy the following year – but the visitors still came.

On 29 August 1923 the *Southend Standard* reported all-day queues of cyclists and pedestrian 'Bank Holiday makers'. Part-time

74 *Freehold land for sale from 30 shillings a plot in 1908.*

75 *In 1930-1 the first Canvey bridge was under construction, just east of the ferry.*

76 *This busy picture underlines the need for a bridge, which opened in May 1931.*

77 *Traffic flows over the new bridge, a venue for sightseers. The old road is in the foreground.*

78 *A barge passes through the opened bridge, 1932-3.*

ferrymen, it was reported, who attempted to set up special services were jealously fought off by the regulars.

One of the last considerations of the Benfleet Vestry was a request from Canvey for a contribution to the costs of a bridge to the island. That was in 1889. Benfleet refused and it took more than another 40 years before a secondhand bridge from the London Docks spanned the creek.

A Bridge at Last

Drawings of a proposed bridge for the Canvey Urban District Council appeared in the *Southend Standard* on 17 January 1929. The cost was estimated at £15,000.

The opening of that first bridge by Alderman J.H. Burrows on Thursday, 21 May 1931 was a great occasion, especially for those on the Canvey side, where the day was declared a holiday and was celebrated with parties. It was named the Colvin Bridge, after the Lord

79 *The old wooden railway station near the ferry. It burned down in 1903.*

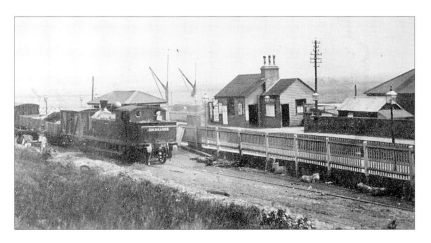

Lieutenant of Essex, Brigadier-General R.B. Colvin, C.B., who had performed the pile-driving ceremony exactly a year to the day earlier.

As a swing bridge, it opened to 60 feet and gave preference to river traffic. Fully laden sailing barges were still able to pass through the creek, causing delays. (I remember walking with my young wife, baby and pram to Canvey on a Sunday afternoon, when overgrown plots with ramshackle buildings still seemed to cover much of the island. On our return we had to wait by the opened bridge to observe the passage of a sailboat.)

The redundant ferryman, Ted Edwards, became the first bridge operator. His portrait is said to have been included as St Christopher by Miss Barbara Nicholson, who painted the chancel or rood screen panels of six male and six female saints in St Mary's church in 1929.

The Colvin Bridge opened for the last time on 26 November 1968. The present permanent bridge was completed in 1973, when the old swing bridge was demolished. 'Ferry Road' is still a poignant reminder of the time when the ferry provided the only access to the island at high tide.

Railways and Commuters

Benfleet's wooden railway station was built near the Canvey Ferry; early photographs show barges lying conveniently alongside it. That station burnt down in 1903, ignited by sparks from a steam engine. (The Downs often caught fire from sparks in dry summers.) The new station was rebuilt nine years later in its present more westerly position at Church Creek.

Where today taxis line up to serve passengers, in 1920 Bill Nunn and Cliff Hart would patiently await custom on the high benches of their horse-drawn cabs.

80 *Old signal box and railway staff, c.1905.*

81 *The new station to the west, with Station Terrace and footbridge, c.1914-15.*

82 *Station Approach, now part of the High Street, from the new bridge, c.1918-20.*

83 *Station Road, c.1913. The butcher's shop to the right is now a private house, but the corner shop on the left has changed little. To the right of the cart was a slaughterhouse, almost opposite Miss Howard's school, top left.*

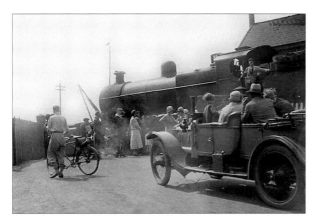

84   *Benfleet Station, 1925-6.*
   left   *Various forms of transport.*
   above left   *A train stops on the level crossing and the train driver has time to chat to people waiting to cross over to Canvey.*
   above   *Level crossing open, viewed from the south.*

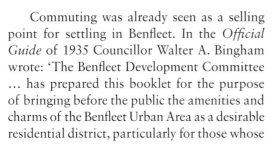

Commuting was already seen as a selling point for settling in Benfleet. In the *Official Guide* of 1935 Councillor Walter A. Bingham wrote: 'The Benfleet Development Committee ... has prepared this booklet for the purpose of bringing before the public the amenities and charms of the Benfleet Urban Area as a desirable residential district, particularly for those whose business or occupation takes them to London or near district and consequently require frequent fast and cheap travelling facilities ...'

The serving stations for the area were: Benfleet and Leigh-on-Sea on the London Midland and Scottish Railway (London terminus Fenchurch Street) and Rayleigh Station on the London & North Eastern line

85   *Motor transport began to replace the horse and the railway sidings replaced the creek in the handling of goods. Jack Polley, left, Fred Edwards, centre.*

86 *Ferry Road, to the south of the railway line, looking east.*

87 *Ferry Road, looking west. On the creekside, Underwoods built motor fishing vessels (MFVs).*

to Liverpool Street for the northern district of Thundersley.

Train services from Benfleet 'to Town' commenced at about 4 a.m. until 10.30 p.m. 'and later in summer'. Rush hour trains between 7 and 10 a.m. were considered 'very frequent' and the service from London ran until after midnight. The return fare by train to Southend in 1937 was 6d. The London return fare was two shillings and threepence.

The road still crossed the rail track at level-crossing gates on its way to Canvey, causing delays. Residential and commercial buildings stood to the west of the High Street where it curves past what used to be the 'Hard' and also to the south between the railway lines and the water's edge. There was even a boatyard, Underwoods, which built motor fishing vessels (MFVs) on the eastern end.

Relations between the 'Iron Horse' and the real thing were not always congenial. On 15 January 1903 the *Southend Standard* reported that Dr Grant, returning from Canvey with his

88 *H.C. Dutton, Railway Approach (with the new railway footbridge), c.1913. By 1925 Duttons had become the Cash Drapery Store.*

horse and trap, found the level-crossing gates closed. For a time the horse waited patiently, then shied at a passing train and dashed into the wharf wall. The doctor was fine, but the horse died shortly afterwards.

In November 1961 electrification began and full service started in June the following year.

An underpass under the railway station resolved the level-crossing problem when it was opened on 5 February 1962. To accommodate it, the dwellings and businesses that had crowded along the water's edge, mainly on stilts, had to be demolished. It also spelled the end of Church Creek, life blood of the commercial hub of Benfleet's marine activities since Saxon days.

89   *Ten years later it was Shiner & Holmes, High Class Drapers (with photographic studio – the photographer was brother of Ronald Shiner, the actor). Today it is a car showroom for four-wheel-drives and scooters.*

90   *Benfleet's level crossing, photographed on 22 July 1958 from the Southend side. On the right is the end of a group of railway cottages, which have since been demolished.* (Reproduced from 'Barking to Southend' (Middleton Press)

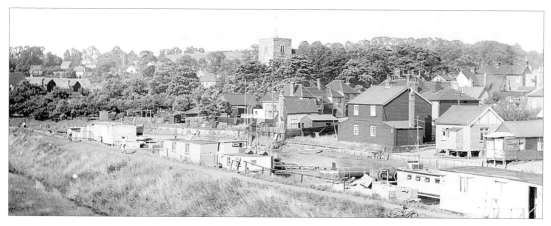

91 *As the creek's maritime connection diminished in the late 1920s, for a while it became a haven for houseboats and, as the railway station was so convenient, the 'Hard' filled up with numerous buildings on stilts. Upsons Estate Agents' hut became tea rooms and the last hut on the far right was used for tyre trading. At some time there were also a lady hairdresser and an Auction Room/ Granary.*

Post Offices

By the 1920s the Post Office had moved from Station Road and was part of the *Anchor* public house. At one time it served the population from Simon Daines' cottage, the site of which, abutting the churchyard, later became the Institute Hall. Miss Henderson must have been mistaken when she remembered the former 'baker', Mr Daines, who lived in a cottage by the creek with his son Jimmy, the one-armed

92 *The area of the previous view seen from the High Street looking north. First left, the semi-detached house of the Killingbacks; next Nurse Revell, who delivered most of the infants in the village. She is still remembered as 'always dressed in black and riding a bicycle'. Then the house of Mrs Wheeler (in 1922 it had been Gladwin). Those houses have gone. The* Hoy *still advertised Livery Stables. The black weatherboarded house, right, was Bill and Marie Nunn's in c.1932. At one time a gents barber and shaver operated from there.*

93 *Crown stables in the centre of this evocative view from the creek, 1915-20. The sawmill, Hoy, Anchor and Crown – and the horse still rules.*

postman. (*White's Directory* stated in 1848 that letters were dispatched at 2.30 p.m. via Rochford.)

After Charlie Brand closed his shop at the *Anchor*, the premises were let to Sid Lawrence and his daughters and that became the Post Office. J.G. Lawrence, of 'The Post Office', published multi-image picture postcards of South Benfleet. Daughter Jane continued as post mistress following their father's death and Mabel was headmistress until she retired, when she added a lending library to their activities. They both lived at the *Anchor*, where the reading folk of Benfleet could borrow books for tuppence a week. A Mr Pratt took over the Post Office in 1950. Since then it was moved close to the churchyard, east on the High Road, and now it can be found at the Co-op on the Parade.

Hopes Green Post Office moved to the parade of shops when that was built in 1928.

Road Systems

Surveyors' accounts ended in 1834. The following year a Highway Act was passed and the office of Surveyor could be abolished.

94 *The High Street in 1903. From the left, the Hoy, smithy and the houses on the churchyard, the Institute and the Anchor. (In 1908 the Anchor Inn still advertised 'Horses and Traps on Hire'.) Front right is the wall of the Crown stables.*

95   *A proud moment in history. The motor car has arrived. A Peugeot in front of the* Anchor, *c.1907. The only lady is May Land of the* Anchor. *Far right is newsagent Fred Knightley. Slightly in front, wearing his bowler hat, stands R. Francis, farmer, first chairman of the Horticultural Society in 1920.*

96   *Fred Knightley (newsagents and tobacconists) and his daughter Doris. In the middle distance are the smoking chimneys of Bridge Houses in North Street, now High Road. Right is the* Anchor. *It must be 1908-10. World affairs intrude into Benfleet village. The 'leader board' reports a meeting between Asquith and the King of Portugal.*

Benfleet's slopes caused problems. In 1900 notice boards had to be placed on Bread and Cheese Hill and on Vicarage Hill, warning of dangers to cyclists on their penny-farthings!

With the increasing importance of the motor car, the days of the horse were numbered, though early in the 20th century all three of Benfleet's hostelries still offered horses for transport.

Originally the overland route from London ran via Pitsea to Jotmans Lane and Hopes Green, to the church and the area of the War Memorial, which was called The Cross. When the A13 connecting Southend to London made that route more viable, the link road to Tarpots from Cemetery Corner became important. The road from the War Memorial to Tarpots had first been called North Street, then London Road. Since 1932 it has been the High Road.

In 1926 the sharp dip in the road where the creek still reached between the churchyard and Hall Farm was filled in and built up, replacing the bridge.

For some people the state of the roads could not improve fast enough. On 5 January 1928 the *Southend Standard* reported a Rochford

97　*Thundersley Park Road, c.1920.*

98　*'Elm trees were everywhere in Benfleet.' The distinctive house in the previous picture of Thundersley Park Road, can be found centre right in this pleasant scene of c.1920.*

99 and 100 *Fred Knightley and his bicycle in Endway; behind him the five-bar gate takes us further downhill into East Street, c.1921. This is now Essex Way.*

Rural District Council application to 'take over and make up Thundersley Park Road', under the Private Street Works Act of 1892, before Southend County Justices. It was refused.

The South Benfleet Ratepayers Association at their monthly meeting, also in January 1928, protested at the speed of motor omnibuses along the London Road (now High Road). Warnings of excessive speeds were raised and 35 miles per hour were mentioned. Equally debated was the dangerous overloading during rush hours. Not much seems to have changed since then. Other voices hinted that it was not only the buses that speeded, but private vehicles as well.

The following month Major Pearse's buses and Westcliff Motor Services Ltd were asked to co-ordinate timetables and the Council was urged to put up road names, so that people would not have to waste journeys finding their way on the muddy roads.

On 29 August 1929, amidst talk of the anticipated 'new Authority', a loan of approx. £7,000 was raised for the making up of Tarpots Road.

101   *Round House and water tower, Vicarage Hill, c.1913. A twin to the octagonal house still survives in Benfleet Road.*

Essex Way would seem a natural route to Hadleigh and Rayleigh to us today, but then the first part was called East Street, which further along became a country lane called the Endway, before going on to a kissing gate near the present Norwood Drive. From there it continued as a footpath to meet with Vicarage Hill at a point marked by what was formerly the Southend Water Company water tower (now Essex FM broadcast tower).

This route seems so obvious today, that it is mystifying why it was not used earlier instead of the narrow, winding Vicarage Hill, which was steeper even than today, unless it derives from Manor Farm in Benfleet's earliest days.

Only in 1937-8 was the road built out to the high ground and renamed Essex Way, with its stunning views over Benfleet, the Seaview Estate and the Downs, to the Thames and the industrial silhouettes along its banks to the west.

Village Community Life

While elsewhere Benfleet was expanding through the railway and the influx of new people, village life still largely revolved around the traditional centre. Most shops were still concentrated in the High Street, around the *Hoy, Crown* and *Anchor*. Today the space once called 'The Cross' leaves the War Memorial isolated in busy traffic. What used to be the hub of the village is just a busy T-junction, connecting Canvey Island, Essex Way and the High Road. A horse trough of 1911 was removed to Cemetery Corner in the 1950s.

To the east, beside the *Anchor* with the Post Office and Library, stood weatherboarded 'Five Elm Cottages', behind the elm trees that can be seen on early photographs. A large space

102   *The path to the water tower, now Essex Way, 1919-20.*

103 *The High Street early in the 20th century, evidence of neglect in wartime. The smithy, beside the Hoy, is still advertising ploughs. The large brick building in centre right is Tuffields Stores (now the Benfleet Tandoori). Downhill on the right is: W.H. Attwell ironmongers shop – carpenter, wheelwright and decorator. Gray's sweet shop advertised Adkins Nut Brown Tobacco. Last on right is the picket fence of the Crown.*

104 *Anchor Cottages, also known as Five Elms Cottages, behind the trees that named them, just east of the Anchor, c.1920.*

105 *In 1920 part of today's car park was still used as allotments, the origins of the Horticultural Society.*

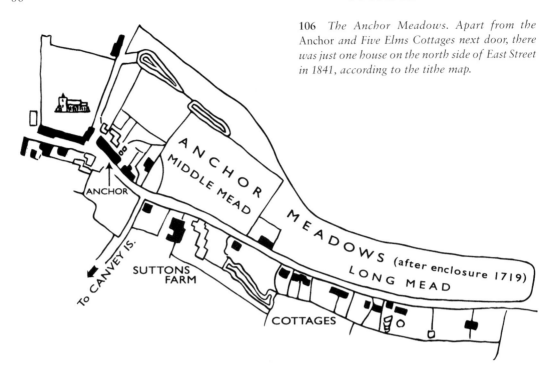

106 *The Anchor Meadows. Apart from the* Anchor *and Five Elms Cottages next door, there was just one house on the north side of East Street in 1841, according to the tithe map.*

107 *Village Fair at the Anchor Meadows, c.1908, part of the Regatta celebrations. Ted Land, landlord of the* Anchor, *directs events.*

108   *Benfleet Regatta, 1908.*

109   *The view from the Canvey side. An early joined-up picture shows crowds on the Downs, on the old station platform, on the water's edge and on the water at the 1910 Regatta.*

opposite the *Anchor*, now part of the station car park, used to be allotment gardens.

Before the National Health Service

In Miss Henderson's memories (1860s-'70s) the village storekeeper, Mr Harridge, also doubled as 'tooth-drawer': 'He sat me on a kitchen chair, stood on another chair behind me, made me throw back my head which he grasped firmly between his knees, told me to open my mouth and extracted the tooth with a pair of pincers, for which I paid him a shilling.'

In the 1920s doctors still called either by horse and trap or on horseback. At black-

110   *King George V*
Silver Jubilee pageant,
6 May 1935. 'Trench
Scene' is a tableau
manned by the
British Legion, South
Benfleet branch, whose
banner now hangs
in Benfleet church.
In the background
are Britannia and her
handmaidens.

111   *'Progress in*
the Film Industry', a
tableau with characters
of the Benfleet
Dramatic Society at
the same occasion.

boarded Killingback's cottage by the creek, the front parlour became Doctor's Surgery twice a week, when Doctor Grant came to see patients. 'There were always people waiting for him outside the cottage on 'doctor days', remembers a local lady.

Another medic, Doctor Wilkes, would come on his rounds on horseback. 'A very smart but fearsome figure he looked, 6ft tall, wearing brown leather riding boots, hacking jacket and riding hat and he usually had a monocle in one eye.'

Village Fairs

The Green behind Hall Farm (today marked by Green Road near the Methodist Church) has been mentioned before as the traditional venue for a toy fair on 24 August every year. At

112 *Church Corner with the War Memorial, late 1930s. Signs of modern times – graffiti on the* Anchor *wall and someone rushing in the direction of the station. Note the boy playing with a diabolo, a two-headed top, two sticks and a piece of string.*

Whitsuntide a travelling Gypsy Fair would be held there, when in the evenings gypsy musicians entertained the village folk.

In the 20th century the fair evolved into the village fête with a new venue on the Anchor meadows. (The meadows along the road to the east of the *Anchor* had been 'taken off the Waste', i.e. enclosed, in 1719 but it was only in living memory that they were covered by bungalows and an electricity sub-station.)

113 *Hall barn early in the 20th century. The houses to the left are in Green Road.*

Benfleet Country Club - -

Brook Road, S. Benfleet.

Telephone: SOUTH BENFLEET 36.

SUBSCRIPTION--5/- PER ANNUM or
1/6 PER QUARTER.
LADIES: 2/6 PER ANNUM.

3 Billiard Tables
Table Tennis
Spacious Lounge
2 Hard Tennis Courts
&c., &c.

THE CLUB HALL—
having a separate entrance and with
seating accommodation for 300
may be hired for Dances, Concerts,
Meetings, &c.
For particulars apply to the Secretary
as above.

MEMBERSHIP of the BENFLEET COUNTRY CLUB is included
in the 2/6 Annual Subscription paid by members of the South
Benfleet Branch of the British Legion.

EX-SERVICE MEN should therefore join the local Branch of
the Legion without delay.

114 *From the Annual Carnival and Fête programme, 1935.*

Benfleet's Regatta was always a spectacle for which the whole village turned out in their finery.

On 6 May 1935 the Urban District celebrated King George V's Silver Jubilee with inter-school sports on South Benfleet Playing Field and a pageant that included the British Legion, the League of Nations' Union, the Salvation Army, the Benfleet Dramatic Society, South Benfleet Women's Institute, Benfleet Chamber of Trade and Commerce, the Fire Brigade and Suffragettes.

August Bank Holiday the same year featured the Annual Carnival and Fête and a procession from Tarpots Corner to the Anchor Meadow with much fancy dress, tableaux, mounted events and a 'Motorcycle Pickle Jar Race', 'Motorcycle Dirty Face Race' and 'Motorcycle

Musical Chairs', not forgetting the 'Married Ladies' Egg and Spoon Race'. 'Water Polo on Land' featured the Benfleet v. Canvey Fire Brigades.

The Smithy, the Institute and Newsagents

Next to the *Hoy* stood the smithy and the skittle alley behind it. The Institute, a small brick and tiled roof building, stood south of the church gate, with Knightleys, the newsagents, to the other side, close to the *Anchor*.

The Village Institute had been purchased by the community in 1892, when the villagers joined together as shareholders in a public company. It had formerly been the property of Simon Daines, but at the time of the village purchase it belonged to James Wilson.

Lantern lectures and penny readings were part of village entertainment when the vicar, the Rev. C.F. Box, hired it. The building served as church hall and concert hall, hosted parties and meetings of Brownies and Sunday School, until, together with Knightleys, it was demolished in 1932 to make room for road improvements. At the same time the High Street downhill was widened. Knightleys took over the living quarters of the Tuffield family and placed a shop window on the ground floor. It is now the 'Benfleet Tandoori'. (As a long-time commuter to London, I remember collecting our 'dailies' from Knightleys news-stand at the railway station before departure.)

In the small village of 1922 we still find, as well as the church and three inns, the school, a blacksmith, grocer, hardware shop, two butchers and a slaughterhouse, cake, fish and sweet shops, a hairdresser, clockmaker, shoemaker, draper, two general stores and two farms.

Benfleet's Hall Barn

Also in 1922, Hall Farm with the unspectacular 'Hall', was still there, with farm pond and barns. Its importance had long since diminished, with absent landlords preferring the revenue from land sales to that of uncertain farming activities. The size of the former tithe barn becomes obvious from old maps. It burnt down in January 1939, after which Walter Bingham described it in the *Parish Magazine* in terms quite difficult to realise today: 'It has stood since the reign of Henry VIII – one of the largest in the county. Cattle and sheep grazed on the adjoining lands.' Howard's Dairy horses were kept in a side barn and escaped the fire when they bolted up St Mary's Drive.

Even the village Green has vanished. At the side of the High Road, one smaller barn survived to within more recent memory.

The Cinema

Benfleet used to have its own cinema on the corner of Brook and High Road; part of the rear of the building later evolved into the Barn Club with billiard tables. A new Benfleet 'Hall' was built in Brook Road in 1922 as a venue for entertainment, such as old people's dinners and dances. By 1936 it had become the Benfleet Country Club and Benfleet Tennis Club made use of the two courts at the rear. Times change and during the war it became first the 'British Restaurant', then a clothing factory. It has since been rebuilt as an old people's home.

The Downs

The lower part of Suttons Farm was enclosed in 1921 under the Town Planning Scheme. Before its demise, the Benfleet Parish Council purchased and secured 30 acres of them on 6 June 1929. Former owner Frank Barnes of Suttons Farm had already allowed public access to the area. On Saturday 14 July 1934, at 5p.m., 'The Downs' were opened for the community by Sir Edgar Bonham Carter, K.C.M.G., on behalf of the Benfleet Urban District Council 'for the use of the public' and is now a part of the Hadleigh Castle Country Park. Councillor and local historian Walter A. Bingham wrote at the time of a view commanding '… a marine history which commenced with the British Coracle, continuing Phoenician and Roman Galley, Norse Dragon, Galleon, Clipper, Benfleet Hoy and the most up-to-date battleship and liner,

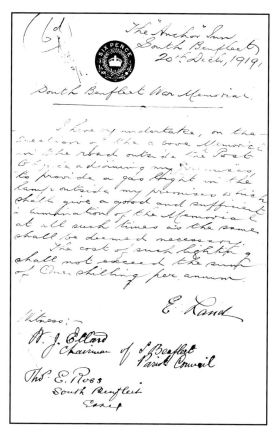

115 *There must have been misgivings about the siting of the War Memorial: a letter from the landlord of the Anchor,* who makes the commitment to illuminate it in the road opposite by gaslight 'at all such times as the same shall be deemed necessary'. Cost not to exceed one shilling per annum.

which have, since the beginning of civilisation passed in review before these Downs.' The event was celebrated with a walk over the Downs by council dignitaries and village folk. It is now a part of the Hadleigh Castle Country Park.

About 1935 the estimated Urban District population was 13,900 in an area of 6,370 acres.

Water

Before 1895 wells at the *Hoy*, the *Anchor* and one at Hopes Green, as well as a few at private

116 *The   Close,
formerly South Street,
is still today lit by gas
lamps.*

117 *Mr Pearse and one
of his coaches.*

118 *A Pearse advert of 1922. W.H. Attwell had become even more versatile.*

119 *Westcliff and Benfleet open-top bus, late 1920s, early 1930s.*

houses and farms, had been the only water supply to the small village. The Parish Council negotiated with the railway company in the hot summer of 1898 and they supplied a tank near the station, which could be replenished, and each household could avail themselves of six buckets of water a day. Access to the pond at the *Anchor* was at first refused by the owners as it was meant for use in the nearby brickfield.

Water supply was regulated by 1903 when mains were being laid in the village. The Rochford Rural District Council announced on 6 April that year: 'Water will shortly be available from their mains in the Parishes of South Benfleet, Hadleigh, Hawkwell, Hockley, Rayleigh and Rochford.' Interested parties were advised to provide themselves with the necessary fittings and apparatus for connection. For domestic purposes only. Others would be charged extra.

Street Lighting

The subject of public street lighting had been raised repeatedly at the Parish Council for some 30 years. Councillor Attwell made a proposal in August 1895 for 12 lamps to be purchased, nine for the village centre and three for Endway. A month later that proposed number was reduced to four by the Parish Council and in another month the whole idea had been thrown out.

120 *Firemen provide a guard of honour for Benfleet's own ambulance, when the* Anchor *was still at the hub of village life, c.1928.*

Resistance to change and the fear of rate rises meant that repeatedly the proposal was voted out – twice in 1898, in May 1901, July 1907 and May 1910. The Grays and Tilbury Gas Company applied to supply the parish in 1912. The following year talk was of it actually happening, but then the Great War kept Benfleet in the dark.

The Lighting Committee of four members of the council looked into the matter again in April 1922. Some residents had lit up their premises privately by then. The first building to be lit by gas was the *Anchor* public house.

In January 1924 the Parish Council made a point of thanking Mr Hackshaw for continuing to light the lamp on his premises at the foot of Vicarage Hill. Resistance was faltering. That year the proposal to adopt the Lighting and Watching Act of 1833 was voted down by only two votes, 45–43.

An agreement was finally reached in June 1926 that 32 lamps would be installed at a cost of £292 17s. 6d. (£292.88p). Extra lamps were ordered in December 1926. In March 1929 the

Chairman of the Parish Meeting reported that five new lamps had been erected during the past year and 'every street or part of a street where gas was available had now been lighted'. It was hoped that there would be electricity 'before many months are over'.

In June 1929 the Parish Council Highways, Ditch and Lighting Committee had a meeting with representatives from the County of London Electric Supply Co. relating to public lighting. Messrs Bingham, Copping, Johnson, Leggett and Littler discussed the conversion of the existing gas standard lamps to electricity and to light the lamps from sunset until 11 p.m. daily. It was anticipated that a supply of electricity to South Benfleet would be available by December that year, but nothing happened and it was decided the old gas lamps should be repaired.

In 1935 the Urban District Council boasted 400 street lamps, lit by gas supplied by the Gas Light & Coke Company Ltd.

Two old gas lamps survive in The Close, renovated at a cost of £500 each, according to the *Evening Echo* of 5 April 1985, and 'beaming out on natural gas'.

Other subjects under consideration in the last years of the Parish Council included a fire service, council housing, the Post Office, raising of the road level behind the *Anchor* towards Vicarage Hill and the sanctioning of private bus services.

In the 1880s, George Land had supplied public transport by horse and carriage from the *Anchor* to Hadleigh. The steep and narrow Vicarage Hill run required four horses.

Brown Buses, Boneshakers and Taxis

Canvey Auxiliary Motors started a bus service in 1919 from Benfleet Ferry to Leigh Beck, which later splashed the ford at low tide to and from Benfleet. On one occasion a broken-down bus was overtaken by the tide and passengers had to be taken off by rowing boat before the water reached roof level.

In 1922 the Benfleet *Parish Magazine* carried advertisements for Pearse's Garage and Motor Works in the High Street, that offered cars and 'blue' charabancs for hire, as well as petrol and accessories. The Benfleet Omnibus Service (The Brown Buses) promised to meet all trains: 'Passengers conveyed to Thundersley, Hadleigh and all roads en route. Cars provided at any time, day and night, for special journeys. Motor Ambulance with stretchers.' The rivalry between Major Pearse's Canvey buses and the Thundersley, Hadleigh and District buses is still remembered by old Benfleetonians.

Before Essex Way was built, buses travelling east had to negotiate steep Vicarage Hill. Passengers occasionally had to alight at the bottom and walk up the hill to re-join the bus on the high ground.

In July 1929 the ambulance service was offered to the Parish Council, who declined the offer, but recommended it to the new Urban Authority.

Benfleet's Fire Brigade

As with street lighting, other things moved slowly in South Benfleet, frugality being the uppermost consideration. At a Parish Council meeting on 10 September 1903 (the year the first railway station burnt down) R. Francis suggested the formation of a Fire Brigade 'to utilise the hydrants, etc., now available through the new water supply'. His idea was to contact various insurance companies for funds to help with accessories. He also assured the meeting that plenty of volunteers could be found.

A brand new bakehouse was opened in South Benfleet in the early 1920s. On the night the new ovens were used for the first time a fire broke out in the bakery and the whole building was gutted.

Ted and George Land and Bill and Bert Blake were among the first fire crew when a voluntary force finally formed in 1924. The Captain was W.H. Shepherd and their hand cart was stored at the *Anchor* stables. A Buick tender was added once sufficient funds had been collected, and the volunteers bought their own uniforms and brass helmets. The official christening of the new appliance was performed by a local doctor's wife, breaking one of the arms of the tender's mascot to the dismay of the proud assembly as she brought down the champagne bottle on the radiator.

The whole village also attended when a local resident donated his garage to house the new acquisition. It must have been a comical sight when eight volunteers, standing inside, lifted and carried the building along the High Road to its new site next to the *Anchor*.

A ship's maroon was set off to call out the crew when an emergency call was made to the *Anchor* and the proud volunteers in their fine brass helmets would rush to man the engine. Ted Land was the driver and his publican brother George would ring the bell 'til he was red in the face'. Ted Land became one of the first full-time firemen together with Harold Layzell.

Of course, such an important service needed a telephone. The Parish Council Finance Committee, at great pains, repeatedly requested the Post Office to supply a list of calls made from the new fire station telephone. That new-fangled device would have been much in demand.

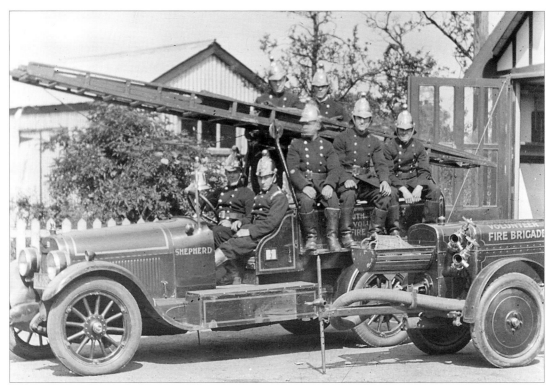

121   *Benfleet's pride, the Fire Brigade.*

122   *When Walter Bingham married Miss Phyllis M.*
Holmes in about 1932, it was as a volunteer member
of the Benfleet Fire Brigade.

The Parish Council agreed a penny rate to
fund the building of a proper fire station in 1928.
It was opened three years later in Hadleigh.
That same year Simonis Limited announced that
South Benfleet had added a 'modern 250/300
gallon Simonis-Thorneycroft self-priming
turbine Motor Fire Engine'.

Early Benfleet telephone numbers may
amuse us today. High Street ironmonger W.H.
Attwell's phone number in 1935 was South
Benfleet 9. Attwells, Purveyors of Meat, had
number 10 and Tuffield's Stores on the High
Street were next with 11. One dialled the *Hoy*
on number 7, but the Leigh Building Supply
Co Ltd on the creek south of the railway lines

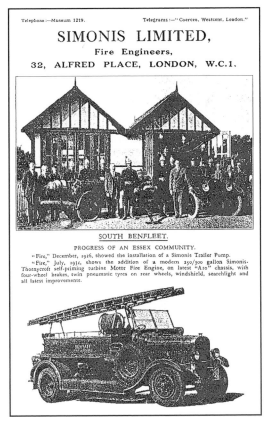

123 *An advert of July 1931.*

124 *Benfleet Road, mid-1920s. A far cry from today's ostentatious confections along that road.*

was ahead with their number 5. F.C. Knightley, Tobacconist, Newsagent and Confectioner's number was South Benfleet 103.

Footpaths and History

Various committees, such as the Lighting Committee and the Footpath Committee, held regular meetings and recorded their Minutes. In June 1922 the Footpath Committee 'recommended that the Parish Council ask the Rochford District Council to erect 'finger posts' to indicate Public Rights of Way on all public footpaths in the Parish ...'.

One fine Sunday morning the *Southend Standard* sent along a reporter and photographer to one of the last official footpath walks by the Committee and members of the public. From 'Bingham's Corner' in the London Road at Hope Road, the route led across Boyce Hill Golf Course to Devil Steps and back from the London-Southend Road near Bread and Cheese Hill, through Hobbly Thick woods, to the Hadleigh-Benfleet Road, 'familiarly known as the Water Tower Road'. Historical associations were pointed out, such as Boyces, 'a farmstead constructed upon the site of an ancient Saxon holding'.

The Devil Steps had only 'in recent years' been provided with concrete steps by the Parish Council. The low ground forming a crescent-shaped plateau used to be an Elizabethan

brickfield. Bricks made there would have been used in the reconstruction of Jarvis Hall and most likely in the brick buttress of St Mary's church. As for the name Devil Steps, it was suggested that 'aspiring and perspiring pedestrians (prior to the concrete steps) had, perhaps, been forced to utter fiery ejaculations fit only for his Satanic Majesty's ears …'.

At Hobbly Thick – or Hobble Thicket – the quantity of hornbeam, 'the sacred wood of the ancient druids', was noted, as well as the reason for the width of a good roadway, which used to be 'a manorial road from the estates of the Appletons for the passage of timber, etc. to the deep creekside'.

There was also comment on relics of ancient earthworks of the Danes and reference to 'the ancient barrows or burial ground of the pre-Saxon settlers, which number three, and are situated on the highest ground of the Benfleet-Hadleigh road on the north side', which seems to have escaped most subsequent historians.

It comes perhaps as no surprise that such interest inspired the proposal 'that a local branch of some society be formed to encourage historical, archeological and natural history research'.

While the love of the area by enthusiastic walkers may be obvious, there was also a sterner side to these rambles: 'to perpetuate the rural footpaths and to prevent encroachment or obstruction', a sentiment both timely and important considering all the new construction going on at the time.

IX

Expansion –
Benfleet's Klondyke

During the building boom of the post-war years, South Benfleet's enlargement began in earnest and much general development and growth took place. The Law of Property Act (1922) abolished all copyhold and quitrents. The system of Council housing started in 1926.

The Vicarage Hill Estate was planned in January 1923, under the authority of Rochford Rural District Council, though until then general planning had been haphazard.

Town Planning at last

According to the *Southend Standard* of 17 January 1929, the South Benfleet Ratepayers Association discussed 'Town Planning' at their monthly meeting at the Council School, London Road (now High Road). Armed with a relevant map, Major P.J. Bowling gave a lecture on the subject, which had only recently been adopted. Not all of the suggestions have materialised, for example, a 100-ft. road from the Endway to Leigh across the Downs. One road built later was also from Endway and would follow 'almost along the lines of the existing footpath to Hadleigh Road' (now Benfleet Road), 'to relieve the traffic on Vicarage Hill'. That road became Essex Way.

It was necessary to coordinate development of the various estates, which hitherto had grown to their own plans. Business areas were scheduled – an area to the south of Jotmans Lane for heavy industry and nearby a portion for light industry. Business areas were planned – just past South View Road and northward

from Croft Road to Tarpots Corner, on the main London to Southend Road near Kents Hill Road and a portion of the Kiln Road.

Residential areas were scheduled for eight, 10 and 12 houses to the acre. (Canvey Island packs in almost double that.)

A further industrial zone was planned on the marsh below the Downs, to the east of the railway station. Formal objections to that idea were entered immediately. Ratepayers' power began to raise its head. In subsequent meetings impassioned speeches were made to forestall such a project that would spoil the views and envelop South Benfleet in 'palls of poisonous industrial fumes'. Luckily for us, the objectors won.

A protest letter was featured in the *Southend Standard* that same month from a 'frontager' of Grosvenor Road, who asked: 'Why this feverish haste?' The Rochford District Council, at the instigation of the Parish Council, were prepared to make up Grosvenor Road. 'The road is of no importance and leads only to undeveloped land. It has not settled down from the upheavals of laying electric mains …' insisted the protester. The prepared sewerage scheme would be much more important …

Older residents still remember how late every Saturday night in the 1920s Mr Milton collected from and emptied the outside privies.

Benfleet Urban District Council

To cope with change, more urban powers were sought by the parishes. The County Council

125 *Benfleet Urban District Council chairman's badge prior to obtaining the Coat of Arms in 1962.*

had long been considering reform and by 1924 amalgamations were certainly on the agenda. A complicated series of negotiations tried to resolve the question of who ought to join whom. Hadleigh with its coach connections to the east had long been in favour of joining Southend because of its infrastructure, notably its sewerage system. The final pattern was not an obvious choice, certainly not for the locals. Ultimately it was a decision made by the County Council, overruling the parishes.

Under the Benfleet and Rayleigh (Constitution of Urban Districts) order 1929, the South Benfleet Parish Council and Thundersley and Hadleigh parishes, formerly of the Rochford District Council, joined to form the Benfleet Urban District Council from 1 October of that year. On 17 September the Parish Council Minutes recorded blandly: '... the balance in the bank to be handed over to the new authority...'

The Urban District was divided into six wards: St Mary's Ward (South Benfleet), Boyce Ward (South Benfleet), Castle Ward (Hadleigh), St James' Ward (Hadleigh), St Peter's Ward (Thundersley) and Victoria Ward (Thundersley).

Councillor Bingham declared in 1935: '... Rapid increase of population, bringing with it needs for closer public health supervision, sewering, road-making, lighting and similar urban services, made the need for alteration of Local Government status imperative.' The sewering system had 'recently been constructed' and was 'most up-to-date'. The Council rate was levied every six months – the rateable value was £79,420.

Public Transport

In 1932 the Bridge family took over the bus route with the green buses of Benfleet and District Motor Services. These alternated every 15 minutes with the red liveried buses of Westcliff Motor Services.

The Eastern National Omnibus Company replaced them in 1952, as well as the Canvey and District Motor Transport Company and the City Coach Company. Southend Corporation Transport and Eastern National joined forces in 1955 until the Transport Act of 1986. The constant advance of the motor car caused more amalgamation when on 29 July 1990 Thamesway Ltd took over most of the Eastern National routes in the area.

126 *Benfleet Urban District Council (1929-30) and their Coat of Arms.*

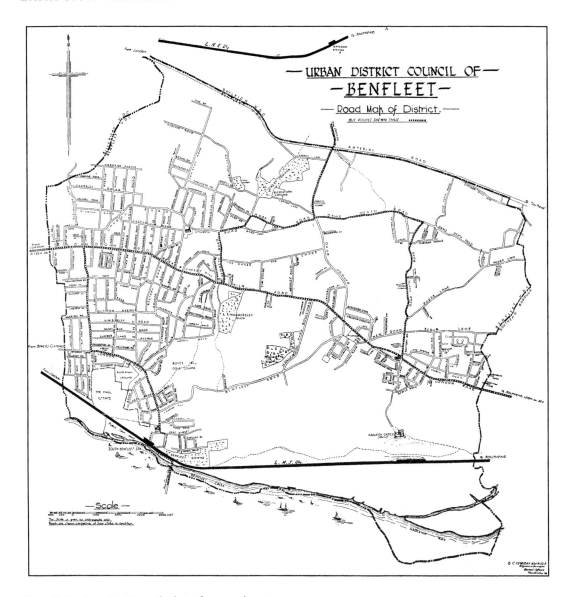

127 *Urban District Council of Benfleet, road map of 1932.*

The New Estates

Major residential developments have given Benfleet a largely urban character, though they reflect the extent of former manors and ownerships.

According to *Kelly's Directory of Essex*, in 1933 the South Benfleet area consisted of 1,949 acres of land, one acre of inland water and 40 acres of foreshore. But, the *Directory* added, ' ... most of the land has now been sold and cut up for building purposes'. Advertisements at the time proliferate with builders' and estate agents' offers and options on 'sweet sites' with 'Bungalows a Speciality'.

A doctor's surgery today stands on the site of Suttons Farm in Essex Way. The years 1927-9 saw a development on the ridge above the Ray, where once Viking lookouts had kept their watch. The Seaview Estate of St Mary's Road,

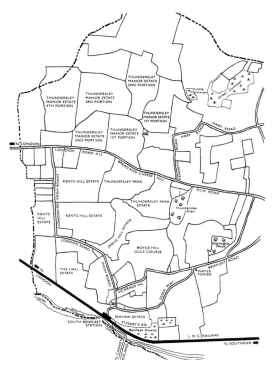

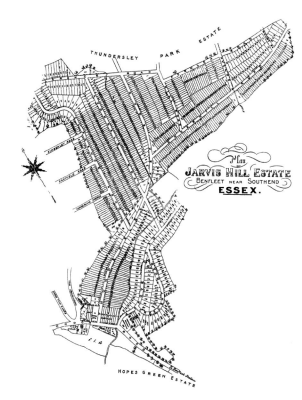

128   *Urban District Council of Benfleet (western section), estate plans of the early 1930s illustrate the march of urbanisation fanning out from the original village by the church to and across the A13 to what is now New Thundersley.*

129   *A detail from previous map shows how the Jarvis Hill estate extended south and across the High Road.*

130   *Tarpots Corner, looking east towards Bread and Cheese Hill, mid to late 1920s. Note the building plots offered for £15.*

131 *Benfleet between the wars: Builders and Estate Agents galore in 1935.*

132 *Vicarage Hill, c.1923.*

133 *London Road, between Green Road and Hope Road, c.1933. Barnes' shop was the first on the left. Before that it was Liberty Market Stores.*

134 *Jackie Barnes and her mother at their shop in the High Road, 1948. Victor Barnes bought the premises in 1950 for £1,300. His parents had rented the bric-a-brac shop ten years earlier.*

135 *Hopes Green, c.1933, looking towards Brook Road on the left.*

136 *High Road in 1925, when it was still called London Road. The shops, Smith Bros. woodyard and pumping station, centre, are still there, but the pumping station is now the Oasis Christian Centre. The new school would be to the right of picture.*

137   *Kents Hill Road, c.1925.*

138   *London Road, now High Road, looking towards Boyce Hill, c.1923. Fred Knightley and his daughter Doris are seen between what are now Wincote Drive and South View Road. The oak tree is still there opposite the bus stop near St Mary's Hall.*

139 Leafy Cemetery Corner, c.1919 – north to Tarpots, right to Hopes Green.

140(a) Greenwood Avenue in the mid-1920s. Not much of the wood was left, but it could hardly be greener.

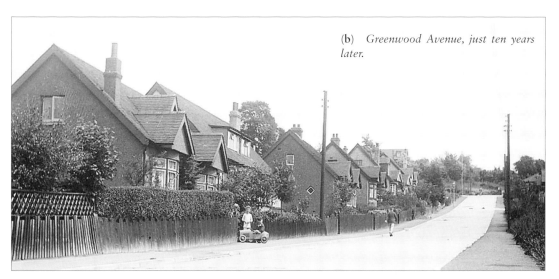

(b) Greenwood Avenue, just ten years later.

Highcliffe Road and Mill Hill was developed by Iversen and Morgan on land sold by Frank Barnes. Mill Hill recalls the post-mill that once stood on the ridge of the Downs.

Estates were spreading to and at Hopes Green, which was no longer a separate settlement. In 1928 the shopping parade at Hopes Green was built and, in the same year, Messrs Raffin and Bonsor built The Parade of shops in the High Road between Richmond Avenue and Kents Hill Road.

In 1914 the South Benfleet Parish Council provided a new cemetery, which gave a name to a sharp bend in the High Road – Cemetery Corner. C.S. Wiggins raised Jotmans Estate at Cemetery Corner in 1936. At that time the Southdown Estate offered semi-detached bungalows for sale freehold at £325 (Cash £315). Repayments were set at £1 13s. 9d. per month.

'Buy your bungalow for 7s. 9d. weekly. ... Total deposit £25!' shouted one firm of building contractors, estate owners and builders.

Much of the building on the new estates was identical. Other estates were developed piecemeal – you found the plot you liked and, usually as a combined offer, the builder would build on it the house of your choice. 'Bungalows and Houses to be Let or Sold or Built to suit Purchaser's requirements' proclaimed another builder in 1935. Walter A. Bingham advertised at about the same time: 'Land for sale on made-up roads with sewering, water, gas, electricity, telephone – near station, trading centre and churches.'

The new estates and developments drew heavily on Benfleet's past when it came to naming the new roads. Grove Road and Brook Road mark one of the Benfleet streams to the creek. Hall Farm Road, Fleet Road, Hope Road, Green Road recall the days of the Manor Farm and the green behind it where the toy fair was held on 24 August each year.

Many Benfleet worthies and old Benfleet families have been remembered in street names on the new estates. Woodham, Tyrell, Appleton, Perry and Watlington were lords of South Benfleet manors. Philmead Road remembers the Benfleet vicar from 1662 to 1680, Geoffrey Philmead. Loten Road honours Robert Loten, hoyman of Hopes Green Farm, who bequeathed the bread charity. Earlier local connections are found in Saxon Way and Danesfield.

X

Wartime and the Post-War Years

In 1913 the word in Benfleet was that at last village evenings would be brightened by gas light. Then came the Great War and the village stayed in the dark until 1926, when street lighting became a reality.

Mr Bingham's garden at the corner of Hope Road and High Road was hit in 1917, when four incendiary bombs were dropped by a Zeppelin. The War Memorial cross was designed by Sir Charles Nicholson and was unveiled in its present position in front of the *Anchor* on 30 May 1920.

In the Second World War Benfleet's geographic position again caused bombs to be dropped by accident rather than by design, when enemy bombers returning from London haphazardly shed any remaining explosive devices. On moonlit nights especially, the gleaming Thames was like a beacon that led the bombers to and from their goal.

At first Essex Way (built 1937-8) was concreted, but its shining surface was such a landmark from the air in wartime, it was quickly tarmaced over. On its flanks, Reeds Hill Farm, just as Boyce Hill Golf Course and every bit of park and land, was taken over by the Ministry for Food and Agriculture, who decided what to sow and plant. George Turner was the Ministry man at Reeds Hill, where Land Army Girls replaced 'up to ten men' that had previously worked the farm.

141 *South Benfleet Special Constables, 1914-18.*

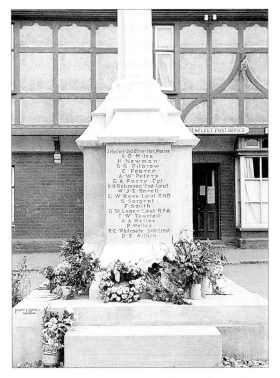

142 *The new War Memorial with the* Anchor *and Post Office.*

The days from 10 July to 31 October 1940 have become known for the Battle of Britain, when Hitler tried to bomb this country into early submission. On 5 September 1940, at 3.30p.m., D. J. Lovell was shot down during combat over the Thames Estuary whilst flying 41 Squadron Spitfire R6885. The aircraft crashed and burned

out at Kimberley Road, South Benfleet. Pilot Officer Lovell of Hornchurch had baled out and was reported safe.

Four days earlier an unexploded parachute mine was found 300 yards from the railway bridge, 40 ft from the railway line, at Jotmans Lane. Train services had to be suspended until the Admiralty rendered it harmless.

Frederick George Toovey, aged 45, of Ivy Cottage, High Street, escaped with 'superficial injuries to his face and head from flying pieces of wood when the roof of Knightleys (the station newsagents) was pierced by bullets when a plane tried to machine gun a train in the railway station' on 9 February 1943.

Some 65 HEs (High Explosives), apart from incendiary bombs, fell on Benfleet and its surroundings between June 1940 and December 1944. Most landed on marshes or fields or gardens, though there was damage to bungalows and houses, occasionally extensive.

The Thames Corridor became known as Doodlebug Alley, but in December 1944 an L.R.R. (Long Range Rocket) or V2 exploded on Boyce Hill Golf Course, a hundred yards from the east of Underhill Road, producing a 49ft x15ft crater. One person was seriously hurt and 13 slightly injured. 40 houses were badly damaged, 101 only slightly. South Benfleet school became a temporary rest centre.

Boyce Hill Golf Course was also the location for an anti-aircraft gun. Incident files on Benfleet start at 9 June 1940 and cease in

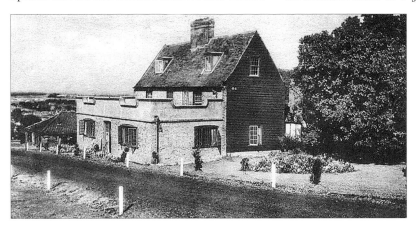

143 *Boyce Hill farmhouse was the first golf clubhouse, with additions, 1927. It became the target for an unexploded bomb in 1941 and was ravaged by fire the following year.*

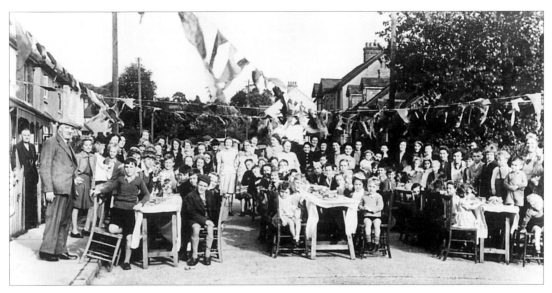

144 *VE Day cele-brations in Hope Road, at the end of hostilities. Jackie Barnes is on the centre table at front left, and her cousin Don Thompson sits opposite.*

145 *Two winter views of Benfleet just 21 years apart, looking from Vicarage Hill towards the church. In 1926 an old wooden cottage stood on the corner site. By 1947 it had disappeared, but Hall Farm buildings still stand on the right.*

December 1944. Towards the end of that period, in 1943-4, several unexploded anti-aircraft shells were recorded.

Disaster of the 'Great Tide'

The night of 31 January 1953 saw the great and devastating east coast floods, which claimed lives and made thousands homeless from Lincolnshire, around Norfolk and Suffolk to Essex. Canvey was particularly badly affected with 58 dead. The whole of the island had to be evacuated. Schools and church halls on the mainland, and even stationary carriages at Benfleet railway station, became shelters for refugees. Benfleet Primary School was the first to open its doors, though quite incapable of accommodating the sheer numbers that arrived, many standing wet and shivering in their only possessions. Volunteers, especially women's organisations, turned out to help with food, tea and warm clothing, and the British Red Cross supplied medical assistance and blankets.

Up on Benfleet Road, a new secondary school, now the King John School, had been about to open the following day, 1 February. The opening was delayed while it became a receiving centre for flood victims.

On Tuesday, 4 February, the Queen Mother and Princess Margaret braved the devastation from the Downs above Benfleet and joined the refugees at the Benfleet Primary School for tea and sympathy, while listening to their stories.

It had happened before. On 15 February 1713 the vicar, Edward Roberts, noted: 'At about six in the evening there blew a violent storm of wind which caused the sea to overflow its banks to the damage of several in this and other neighbouring parishes ...' Again on 16 February 1735-6, while nine parishes still claimed tithes on Canvey, about half the cattle were drowned in a particularly high tide.

After the Second World War building continued. In 1964 the *Southend Standard* reported that in Benfleet 6,088 houses had been built privately since the war and in that year 597 had been completed by the Council.

146   *The Queen Mother and Princess Margaret with victims of the Great Flood at Benfleet Primary School.*

Town Planning was actually implemented, following the Town and Country Planning Act of 1947. In September 1957 the first town map for Benfleet was approved. There was land still available for major residential development in the parishes of Benfleet and Thundersley. In 1949 Benfleet had a population of 19,000. By June 1973 it was up to 43,000.

Land was allocated for industrial development at the Manor Trading Estate, New Thundersley, an area to the south of the Arterial Road (A127) and on the north side of the A13 east of Tarpots. Principal shopping and business areas were restricted to New Thundersley, Tarpots, London Road, Victoria House Corner and adjacent to Benfleet Station.

When Benfleet became a highway authority in 1963 a concentrated ten-year plan was agreed to deal with the problem of unmade roads. Only a handful remain today. Road and junction improvement schemes included Victoria House Corner roundabout and yellow lines were introduced to ease the flow of traffic.

Clubs and Societies

The end of the First World War was like a new beginning for South Benfleet. The building

147 *Adverts from 1935.*

boom with its influx of new people created the need for social and sporting activities. Clubs and societies evolved, generally to great success.

The 1935 *Official Guide* of the Urban District Council boasted of a Golf and Country Club, the Benfleet Country Club, Women's Institute, a branch of the British Legion, Yacht Club, Horticultural Society, Dramatic and Operatic Societies, Tennis, Football, Cricket, Hockey, Bowling, and others, as well as a Ratepayers' Association, Political Associations, Church Guild, a branch of the League of Nations, Masonic Lodge, Girl Guides, Boy Scouts, Sea Scouts and 'one of the most modern Miniature Rifle Ranges' (at the *Anchor*).

The South Benfleet Horticultural Society

This grew out of the wartime 'South Benfleet Food Producers Association' at a Special General and Public Meeting held at the Village Institute at 8 p.m. on Wednesday, 2 June 1920. In January the following year the rules were drawn up at Mrs Woods' schoolroom. There were 125 initial members and membership was set at a minimum of one shilling. Colonel F. Hilder MP was President and Mr R. Francis, retired farmer, was Chairman.

The new society held its first show on Mr Land's Anchor meadows in an 80-ft. marquee. An orchestra played, as well as the Shoeburyness Railway Silver Band and the evening culminated in a dance. Proceeds, including the sale of approximately 300 horticultural exhibits, were in aid of Southend Victoria Hospital. Sports were organised in association with the Benfleet Rovers Social and Athletic Club. A tug of war between youths of Canvey and Benfleet, guessing the number of peas in a bottle, a swing, coconut shies, hoopla and refreshments were all on offer and a photographer and a policeman attended.

Affiliation to the Royal Horticultural Society followed in 1923 and in 1926 to the Rose Society. That year the Show venue was transferred to the newly built South Benfleet Primary School until the hiring out of schools for social functions was discontinued in 1958.

The Society's grounds at Cemetery Corner were leased from undertakers S. Stibbard in 1948 and purchased outright in 1969. The 1952 Summer and Fete Show at South Benfleet Primary School had 166 classes, a Flitch trial, side shows, a concert, dancing, refreshments, auction and 'all the fun of the fair'.

The Council took over procurement of allotments from the Society in 1980.

Benfleet Yacht Club

Keeping alive South Benfleet's historical involvement with the sea, the Benfleet Yacht Club was founded in 1922 and had a succession of floating Headquarters. On 5 January 1928 the

Southend Standard referred to the 'progressive Club' and announced: 'New Headquarters for Benfleet Yacht Club … The Britannia will be towed to Benfleet and moored in a convenient birth nearer the station than the Soar is now'. The *Soar* was a converted Thames sailing barge, a sprittee. Since 1984 Headquarters have been on the Canvey side of Benfleet Creek in more permanent purpose-built premises.

The club has organised the Nore Race since the 1920s, a race around the Nore Light Vessel, four miles south-east of Shoeburyness. It is today 'one of the premier and largest yacht races in the south-east of England', approximately 20 miles, and attracts an average of around 200 entries, from cruisers to dinghies.

Boyce Hill Golf Club

With its origins in the Leigh Park Golf Club at Belfairs Farm, the first meeting of Boyce Hill Golf and Country Club Ltd was held on 3 August 1922. It was decided that Boyce Hill Farm was to be leased for 99 years. Boyces was described as comprising 119 acres of hills and dales, 'with grand views over the rolling hills of Thundersley to the north and west, Thundersley Glen to the east and the river

148 *Benfleet Yacht Club had a succession of floating headquarters. Today the clubhouse stands on the Canvey side across the creek.*

149 *Members of Benfleet Yacht Club at a Dinner in St Mary's Hall, School Lane, in 1956-7, when Stan Cross was Commodore.*

150   *Boyce Hill Golf Club menu cover, 1950.*

V2 rocket landed in the vicinity of the present 15th Hole ladies tee, producing a pond which was later filled in.

At the A.G.M. of 28 June 1948 it was decided to 'put the club back on its feet'. In 1956 a new clubhouse was opened. Dutch Elm disease hit the area especially hard. Over 90 major trees were lost in 1970 and 200 trees in all had to be destroyed. The hurricane of 1987 next took its toll of the new plantings, so that since 1970 some 3,000 trees, large and small, have been replanted.

The Benfleet Hoymen

Morris and Sword Dancers joined together in the early 1950s. In their time they travelled far and wide – even to Teheran, it is rumoured – in pursuit of an audience. The seahorse was their mascot. The group was dissolved again in the 1990s for lack of members.

The Benfleet and District Historical Society

This Society celebrates its 50th anniversary in 2005, for it first met in 1955. The first Annual General Meeting followed in March 1956. There were 74 members and the bank balance was

Thames, together with the quiet villages of Benfleet and the adjoining Canvey Island to the south'.

The course was laid out and fairways cut, so that the first nine holes could be played over on the formal opening day of 1 October that same year. The clubhouse, until 1939, was the original Boyces farmhouse, with some late additions.

An early club handbook mentions the convenience of the railway at Benfleet and the 'leisurely amble through the country churchyard and by a winding path up Vicarage Hill ...'. Without a car, the fresh-air exercise began at the railway station.

During the war an anti-aircraft unit and searchlight were based on the high ground. The clubhouse received a direct hit in 1941. The bomb did not explode, but a large part of the building was destroyed. The following year a fire destroyed the rest. Later in the war a

151   *Benfleet Hoymen in the late 1970s or early '80s at the Cliffs Pavilion, Westcliff.*

152 *H.E. Priestley, M.A., M.Ed., Ph.D., Benfleet historian.*

£11 16s. 7d., 'a substantial sum', as the meeting agreed. The first President was Mr C.P. Kean, manager of Barclays Bank in Benfleet.

One vice-president was Councillor Walter Bingham, 'a very erudite grocer', who has been mentioned before in these pages. An old and prominent inhabitant of Benfleet, he wrote the first local guide and was instrumental in securing the Downs as a public open space. He wrote in the Urban District Guide: '... to have lost to posterity this beautiful space would have been tragedy indeed ...'. The other vice-president was W.T. Phillips, a teacher at Canvey Island, who held classes on local history, first at Thundersley Primary and then at King John School. Dr Harold Priestley (1900-89) was secretary. He made an invaluable contribution to the research into and the recording of the history of Benfleet from early to modern times.

A much-loved man of many talents, the former headmaster at Plaistow Grammar School in East London had been forced to retire in 1950 through ill health. It was Benfleet's gain.

In his *History of Benfleet* he wrote: '... the local historian ... explores in his mind old tracks, fields, hedgerows, watercourses and buildings now vanished, places which are now covered by streets of suburban dwellings and he becomes acquainted with many of the fascinating characters who once lived in the locality.' Dr Priestley has since joined those fascinating characters at 89 years of age, but this writer for one is grateful for his diligence and legacy.

Benfleet Operatic Society

From its beginnings in 1956 as the Benfleet Methodist Choral Society the BOS has developed its varied programme with a mixture of shows, operetta, choral work and concerts. Its first production was *Christmas Music* from Handel's *Messiah*. Dick Guy was the organist and Marian Mitchell took the baton, a post she held almost continually until her death in 1995.

Later the Society changed its name to Benfleet Operatic Society and in 1970 moved from the Methodist Church to larger premises at the Appleton School Theatre. The repertoire extends from Handel's *Passion Music* and Gilbert and Sullivan's *The Sorcerer* to oratorio and Savoy operas. In the 1970s grand opera was staged with excerpts from *The Marriage of Figaro* and *Don Giovanni*.

Benfleet Camera Club

A handful of original members first met in June 1966 in the back of Don Reed's photographic shop in Benfleet High Road. The Benfleet and District Photographic Club, as it was then called, soon outgrew that small space and the ten or so enthusiasts moved to the Benfleet Junior School along the High Road.

This, too, was found wanting, not least because of the size of school seats designed for seven-to-ten-year-olds. This writer can

153 *Members of Benfleet Camera Club in the 1990s. From left: Ken Hegan, Ralph Taylor, Martin Barnard, Frank Tomkins, Ray Davis, Bryan Burns, Rod Liddel. Kneeling: Robin Miller.*

vouch for the discomfort, as it marked his first attendance. At the 1968 AGM it was decided to shorten the name to the Benfleet Camera Club.

Numbers grew rapidly and, for six years from 1968, meetings were held at the small halls at the rear of Runnymede Hall.

In 1974 the club moved to a brand new hall at the John Burroughs Recreation Ground in Hadleigh until 1989. The present address is St George's Church Hall in Rushbottom Lane.

XI

The Twentieth Century
and Beyond

Benfleet's expansion is demonstrated by the catchment area for Benfleet Horticultural Society membership. In 1920 it was a five-mile radius from St Mary's church (excepting Canvey Island); it became a five-mile radius from Cemetery Corner in 1951 and from Tarpots Corner in 1952. In 1956 membership was opened to all in the Benfleet Urban District Council area and since 1965 it has been open to all.

The Estate That Never Was

Thankfully the open vista to either side of the Essex Way has been retained. The 1935 Carnival and Fête Programme featured a 'merely informative' fold-out map of a new planned estate. The Reeds Hill Garden Estate would have covered the Downs from Vicarage Hill to the north, Norwood Drive to the west and from the Water Tower south. It contained an hotel, cinema and shops. A continuation of St Mary's Road would have eventually joined with the southern extent of the new conurbation. 'Why not come and live near the Sea? It's no dearer than a London Suburb,' proclaimed a strapline.

The idea was revived in 1948. Essex County Council rubber-stamped it, but the borough engineers insisted that the land was unstable and Southend Water Company were worried about the water tower. Work started in 1950. Land movement soon proved the engineers right and Southend Water contacted their legal department. Only the Anchor meadows and

Norwood Drive were built. Today road edgings on Essex Way still indicate the side streets that had been planned along its route.

The 'big house' on Reeds Hill had been pulled down just before the Second World War, presumably to make room for the new estate – the estate map does not allow for a farm. 'There were orchards here and gardens, a well and a pump house', points out today's farmer. It was a big house. The cellars and the well have been filled in. After the War the house was not allowed to be rebuilt, probably for the same reason that the estate building was halted. Today's farmhouse is a single-storey house away from the original complex, but with grand views.

Tarpots Hotel was built early in the 20th century. On the opposite corner the last remnants of the old Tarpots farm were taken down in the early 1950s to make way for a petrol station and car sales firm. (At the moment of writing there is talk of them being replaced by another supermarket.) Also on the south side of the road, Little Tarpots farm stood between New Park Road and Kents Hill Road, straddling the border with Thundersley parish – the parish border passing through house and pond.

Changes in the 1960s

More cottages on Essex Way were demolished in 1961. Originally they had been poor houses which were sold by the parish in 1843. Only 'the Moorings' at the corner of Grosvenor Road survives. In turn the cottages replaced

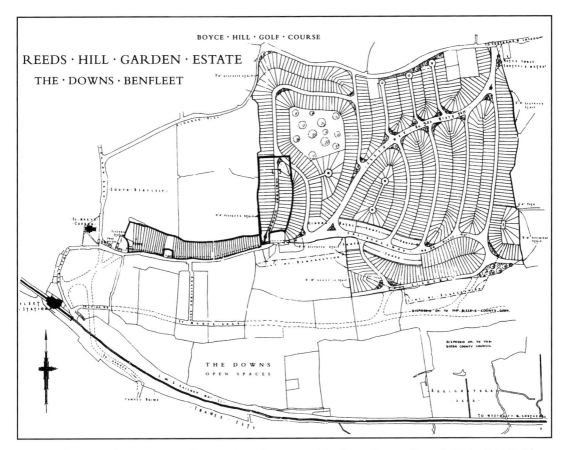

154 *The estate that never was. This map is rubber-stamped by Essex County Council, 30 April 1949. The small area outlined in black was actually built. Water Tower at top right, railway station far left. A cinema, hotel and shops were pencilled in. Note the proposed roads across the car park. (First published with the Carnival and Fête Programme, August Bank Holiday 1935.)*

155 Tarpots Hotel, *early to mid-1930s.*

156 *Old cottages, East Street, at the corner of Grosvenor Road. The former poorhouses had been sold by the parish in 1843. Most were demolished in the 1960s, with only the farthest, 'The Moorings', surviving.*

157 *A former occupant of the demolished cottages, probably of the 'Clubb' family.*

an earlier poor house on the churchyard that Benfleet shared with Thundersley parish. The Vestry Book shows that in the 18th century the rent from the nearby smithy helped to pay for its upkeep.

The railway underpass opened on 5 February 1962, spelling the end of the historic creek. By the creekside 'Paynes Cottages', once the homes of the Killingbacks and Nurse Revell, were sold to Essex County Council in August 1960 before demolition. 'Wharf Cottage', by the *Hoy and Helmet*, very likely succumbed to a similar fate. Those houses did not exist in 1846 and were probably built to accommodate residents displaced by the railway. Similarly, the houses that survive opposite the creek near the

158 *Church Creek, late 20th century.*

Half Crown, such as Belle View, Ivy and Rose Cottages and Rosedale and Felicitie (the latter two have become a single home since) date from that time, more than 150 years ago. Then the area was part of Henry Wood's estate. By the 1960s much of the space between the Alley and the High Street belonged to Frederick John Leach of Waterside Farm, Canvey. At his death in January 1966 more of the land and dwellings became available and tenants were given the option to buy.

In 1968-9 the Benfleet Conservative Club was founded and acquired several of the cottages along the Alley, now 'The Close'. One of the cottages was added to and extended westward to the High Street to create the modern premises, but including the original cottage, its fireplace and a mysterious set of wall panels painted in a classic Italian style. The wooden panels possibly have a connection to the resident ghost, thought to be that of Lady Hamilton, Horatio Nelson's controversial Emma.

159 *By the 1950s the* Hoy *had become the* Hoy and Helmet *and at the creekside, close to today's larger version, stood Clarke's shellfish, jellied eels and oysters stall. Mr Clarke came here in 1948-9, when his old site was incorporated in the building of the Conservative Club. This picture was taken in the early 1950s, when the Austin A30 was new. The smithy, far right in this picture, had become an electrical store before it made way for car parking.*

160 *'Fellowship will blossom'. Armorial bearings were granted to Castle Point Borough Council in 1987. Under the Local Government Act 1972, which came into force from 1 April 1974, the former Urban District Councils of Benfleet and Canvey Island were abolished and the area previously governed by these Councils was to be controlled by the new Castle Point Borough Council. The new Coat of Arms combines elements of its predecessors. The red third that stood for the Royal Honor of Thundersley and the green third of Hadleigh's royal park now symbolise urban and rural areas. The blue and white waves that represented the creek now embrace the Thames around Canvey. The motto 'Societas Florebit' means 'Fellowship will blossom'. As horns on Viking helmets were only a Victorian invention, it is pleasing to see that they have been dropped from the new Arms.*

At the end of the Alley, and almost behind the modern car showroom, stood the Old House of Benfleet, the five-bedroom, black-weatherboarded home of the Hayklan family. 'Mama' Hayklan painted under the name of Elizabeth Cochrane and drew cartoons for the *Daily Sketch*. The atmospheric house and its family made way for the western exit of the station car park, when that was enlarged and tarmaced in the 1960s. Yet the Alley remains a tangible link to Benfleet's past.

With its importance as a thoroughfare to the station and to Canvey Island, the High Street was further widened in 1966, when more houses were demolished between the *Anchor* and the *Hoy and Helmet*. The narrow green

161 *Chairman of the Council, Ron Williams, with the Benfleet Carnival Queen and her entourage at the Runnymede Fayre early in the 1980s.*

strip between road and churchyard wall today seems an impossible space for houses, but Charley Tingey had his cycle and rifle shop here and upstairs his flame-haired wife Lily looked after her Tea Rooms. Grace and Dorothy Anderson kept a hairdressers from 1930-45. Lucy Marshall's florists became a chemist shop before its demise. For a time the smithy was transformed into an electrical shop.

More Amalgamation – The Castle Point Borough Council

A blue ribbon was cut on 14 April 1962 by the Lord Lieutenant of Essex, Col Sir John Ruggles-Brise, Bt, C.B., O.B.E., T.D., J.P., at the opening of the £80,000 block of offices intended to house all departments of the Benfleet Urban District Council, instead of two previous buildings. The Lord Lieutenant mentioned the playing fields, nature reserves, shopping centres, recreation grounds and now the Council offices 'worthy of your 32,000 people …'

Runnymede Hall was officially opened by Councillor R.M. Williams, Justice of the Peace, on 10 December 1965. The former council offices to the west in Kiln Road are now a Council Health Centre.

The Benfleet Urban District Council's amalgamation of South Benfleet, Thundersley and Hadleigh parishes had been described as a shotgun wedding between reluctant partners. In 1974 they joined the administration of Canvey Island District Council and together they formed Castle Point Borough Council with 39 elected members. The Local Government Act of 1972 came into force from 1 April that year. A public competition produced the name Castle Point, which embraces the area from Hadleigh Castle to Canvey Point.

The new offices were considerably enlarged and in 1992 any staff still located on Canvey were brought from the island to the Kiln Road offices. HRH the Princess Royal unveiled a stone of commemoration for the new centralised Council Offices on 27 February that year. A nuclear shelter is part of the foundation of the modern premises.

At its demise in spring 1974, the Urban District Council owned 976 houses, of which 219 had been erected in the previous seven years: 564 of them were three-bedroomed houses and 270 were occupied by senior citizens.

St Mary's 1100th Anniversary was celebrated on 9 July 1994 with a pageant at Richmond Playing Fields, involving historical recreations,

162 *St Mary's 1100th Anniversary programme, 1994.*

choirs, players from all the Benfleet schools with a programme of events and concerts.

Benfleet Library used to be in Elim Church Hall. When Barclays Bank on the corner of Green Road and High Road closed, the Library moved in temporarily, until on 21 June 1995 brand new premises on the corner of Constitution Hill and Thundersley Park Road, formerly the site of 'The Limes', were opened by HRH the Duchess of Gloucester.

Millennium Population

Late in the 20th century, in 1991, South Benfleet's population was estimated at 15,000, part of the 84,900 for Castle Point Borough. By 2004 Benfleet was estimated at 15,150, with 87,000 for the Borough. The numbers roughly divide equally, with 50 per cent of the population living on Canvey Island and 50 per cent in the rest of Castle Point.

Today Castle Point has about 90,000 residents and the highest proportion of owner-occupiers of all UK constituencies (about 90 per cent).

Looking to the Future

Since 1988 the old village centre of South Benfleet (close to the former creek) has been designated a Conservation Area, to protect what is left of the historical heritage of the village, yet vigilance is still paramount. As recently as September 1995 an attempt was made by developers to fill in the creek and cover that ancient area to the west of the church with another development of 26 houses. Local people took up the gauntlet and protested until the proposal was rejected.

Except for small pockets of 'infill' or redevelopment for more modern and spacious housing, Benfleet's expansion has probably reached its limits. Its proximity to London, to the Thames and the views from the Downs make it a favoured place to live. Indeed, on the lofty ground of Benfleet Road and the green exclusivity of Vicarage Hill, property prices can easily exceed one million pounds.

163 *Father Michael Galloway, parish priest, addressing assembled participants on playing fields that used to be marshland, across the creek from the church.*

164 *A latter-day Viking, one of the children of St Mary's at the pageant.*

The north door of St Mary's church, which had been filled in for centuries, has been opened up again in 2005 to allow access for wheelchairs. That architectural marvel, the beautiful south porch, is again scheduled for repairs.

Also in the summer of 2005, Castle Point Borough Council applied for and received a business grant of £50,000 to develop a memorial to the Battle of Benfleet. Two artists have been commissioned to create four sculptures that will be themed around the battle, with the involvement of the local community. The site is on Council land west of St Mary's church and the former Church Creek.

The population of Canvey Island has grown to such an extent that the islanders are again clamouring for their own administration. In 1994 re-organisation of local government was under review by central government, with more 'unitary councils' envisaged. It was proposed that Castle Point, with its population of 87,000, should join with one (or more) of its neighbours. For example, Basildon has a population of 162,000, Rochford of 76,000, Southend 165,000 and Thurrock 129,000.

Southend and Thurrock are now Unitary Councils, which means that, in addition to their original areas of responsibility, they have taken on the responsibilities previously undertaken by the County Council, such as schools, libraries, social services, and the rest. The other District and Borough Councils, including Castle Point, have been left to run as before under Essex County Council.

As if to underline changing times and climate, at the top of the appropriately named Greenwood Avenue, on a hillside sheltered by remnants of former forests, a tropical garden has been privately developed, adding quite a new dimension to the former lands of Westminster Abbey and the Appletons.

165 *South Benfleet and the Thames at Hole Haven with Essex Way.*

Bibliography

Benton, Philip, *The History of Rochford Hundred, vols. I-III* (1867)

Bingham, Walter A., *Benfleet, a Guide and History of the District*, Urban District of Benfleet, Official Guide (*c*.1935)

Brown, A.F.J., *Essex People 1750-1900 from their diaries, memoirs and letters*

Brück, Helga, Hallmann, Robert and Galbraith, David, *John Christian Mantel - Johann Christian Scheidemantel (1706-1761)*, Erfurt (1998)

Chisman, Norman M., *Bygone Benfleet* (1991)

Dawe, Donovan, *Organists of the City of London 1666-1850* (1983)

Defoe, Daniel, *Tour through the Eastern Counties of England* (1722)

Deutsch, Otto Eric, *Handel: a documentary biography*, Adam and Charles Black (1955)

Domesday Book, vol. 32 Essex (John Morris, ed. 1983)

Fawcet, Trevor, *Music in eighteenth-century Norwich and Norfolk* (1779)

Foster, Joseph (ed.), *Alumni Oxonienses* (1715-1886) and (1891)

Friends of Historic Essex, *Essex Freeholders Book, 1734* (1982)

Heygate, Rev. W.E., *Memoir of the Rev. J. Aubone Cook, Vicar of South Benfleet* (1860)

Jarvis, Stan, *Essex, A County History* (1993)

McCave, Fred, *History of Canvey Island* (1985)

Mann, Dr. A.H., *Essex Musical Events and Musicians*, Norfolk Record Office (MS 448)

Mann, Dr. A.H., *Great Yarmouth Musical Events*, Norfolk Record Office (MS 442)

Morant, Philip, *History and Antiquities of the County of Essex* (1763-1768)

Neale, Kenneth, *Essex in History* (1977)

Pevsner, Nikolaus, *The Buildings of England - Essex* (1965)

Priestley, H.E., *A History of Benfleet, Early Days*, Castle Point Borough Council (1977)

Priestley, H.E. and Phillips, Wyn T., *A History of Benfleet, Book* Two, *Modern Times*, Castle Point Borough Council (1984)

Reaney, P.H., *The Place Names of Essex* (1935)

Schlager, Karlheinz, *Repertoire International des Sources Musicales, vol. 5* (1975)

Tickell, Ian, *Boyce Hill Golf Club, A Short History* (2000)

Other Sources:

Anglo Saxon Chronicle (BL MS Cotton Tiberius A. vi, folios 24 recto and 24 verso)

Benfleet Urban District Council (various publications)

British Library (various documents and publications)

College of Arms

Essex Record Office (various documents and publications)
Greater London Record Office
Grove's Dictionary of Music and Musicians
Guild Hall Diaries (various)
Kelly's Directory of Essex (various editions)
Muniment Room and Library, Westminster Abbey (145756 Surveys, valuations, terriers of S.B.
      Parish and Manor, 1771-1856) and (Church Commissioners Records)
Music Department of St Paul's Cathedral
Norfolk Record Office
Public Record Office (The National Archives)
Royal Commission on Historical Monuments in London Vol. V, East London (1930)
South Benfleet Parish Magazine (Early editions, St Mary's Church, now ERO)
Southend Evening Echo
Southend Library Local Studies
Southend Standard (early editions)
Victoria County History, Essex

Index